Freefall to Fly

A BREATHTAKING JOURNEY TOWARD a LIFE of Meaning

REBEKAH LYONS

LifeWay Press® • Nashville, Tennessee

Published by LifeWay Press®
© 2014 Rebekah Lyons

Freefall to Fly © 2013 by Rebekah Lyons. Published by Tyndale House Publishers;
Carol Stream, IL. Used by permission.

ISBN 978-1415-8777-46
Item 005558690
Dewey decimal classification: 248.843
Subject headings: WOMEN \ DEPRESSION (PSYCHOLOGY) \ CHRISTIAN LIFE

To order additional copies of this resource, write to LifeWay Church Resources,
Customer Service, One LifeWay Plaza, Nashville, TN 37234-0113; fax 615.251.5933;
phone 800.458.2772; order online at www.lifeway.com or email orderentry@lifeway.
com; or visit the LifeWay Christian Store serving you.

Printed in the United States of America

Adult Ministry Publishing, LifeWay Church Resources,
One LifeWay Plaza, Nashville, TN 37234-0152

Contents

About the Author

...

Rebekah Lyons is a mother of three, wife of one, and dog walker of two, who recently relocated from New York City to Nashville, Tenn. She's an old soul with a contemporary, honest voice who puts a new face on the struggles women face as they seek to live a life of meaning. Through emotive writing and speaking, Rebekah reveals her own battles to overcome anxiety, depression, and consumer impulses—challenging women to discover and boldly pursue the calling God has for them. As a self-confessed mess, Rebekah wears her heart on her sleeve, a benefit to friends and readers alike.

Alongside her husband, Gabe, Rebekah serves as cofounder of Q Ideas, a nonprofit organization that helps Christian leaders winsomely engage culture. Her favorite pastime is spent with her nose in a book and a discriminating cup of coffee in hand.

To hear more of Rebekah's story, read the entire book, *Freefall to Fly: A Breathtaking Journey Toward a Life of Meaning* (Tyndale House Publishers).

Introduction

As much as we tried to keep things light, a heaviness hung in the air, ready to descend upon the first moment of delayed silence. You can't get through a night like that without a wave of emotional delirium crashing into a sea of tears. Memory lane took an awkward turn into terms of endearment, but still none of us wanted to admit the real reason for our gathering.

We were saying good-bye.

Thirteen years earlier, my husband and I had moved to Atlanta from Virginia. Recent college graduates. Newlyweds. Armed with eager idealism, we found in Georgia everything we were looking for: a church where we made our faith our own, dream jobs that gave permission for our natural talents to soar, a community that celebrated every milestone as a family. Yet our time was not without struggle.

Our first son, Cade, was born with Down syndrome. A dear friend died of a heart attack in my husband's and another friend's grasp. Moments of bliss were accompanied by moments of tragedy. We pressed into each other as we walked one day at a time.

These people and this city had become my home. My family. My safety. My security. Some of my life's greatest questions had been answered here, and I had established a routine. Margin existed for preparing healthy meals for my three kids, infrequent scrapbooking, dabbling in sewing and DIY projects, hosting celebrations ranging from egg hunts to summer cookouts. Everything seemed perfect. As it should be.

Leaving everything behind and moving to New York City did not come easy. In fact, my journey would include a crash and burn—a wrestling match with God that took place in the years and months and weeks and days prior to moving.

God had made it clear that this was something we were supposed to do, but there was a lot of ambiguity around what that meant and what it would look like. We were taking our three children (at the time they were 9, 7, and 5) from the suburbs of the South to the city of the North and so much would change.

Looking back, I had marched off to the Big Apple armed with eager idealism in search for meaning. But instead, I found surrender.

Today, I realize meaning follows surrender. But here I go getting ahead of myself ...

Take a moment to watch the introductory video, "The Crash & Burn," by author Rebekah Lyons, available for free at *www.lifeway.com/freefall*.

CHAPTER 1

...

Life Unsettled

It's God whispering: I am here.

I am true. I am strength. I love

you as you are. Broken and

fragmented. Let Me carry you.

Let Me show you a life you

never dreamed or imagined.

I cry out to God Most High, to God who fulfills his purpose for me.
PSALM 57:2

You have made us for yourself, O Lord, and our
heart is restless until it rests in you.
SAINT AUGUSTINE'S *CONFESSIONS*[1]

Unsettled

...

adapted excerpts from the prelude and Chapter 1 of Freefall to Fly

If you haven't already, take a moment to watch the introductory video, "The Crash & Burn," by author Rebekah Lyons, available for free at *www.lifeway.com/freefall.*

Sunshine pierced the sky the day the restlessness began. My husband, Gabe, had just finished giving a talk on "engaging culture" at Trinity Grace Church on Manhattan's Upper West Side. We left our kids with their grandparents in Atlanta for the weekend, freeing us to bask in the city's glow.

Though we had never considered living in New York, the city represented hallmark moments in our relationship—our first kiss in front of the Rockefeller Center Christmas Tree and, eighteen months later, a fairytale weekend when Gabe asked me, on bended knee, to marry him. The "Big Apple" was a fantastical city of lights, but it became a place of celebration for us, far removed from laundry lists and grocery shopping and paying bills. The thought that the two worlds might collide sounded crazy. Good thing we were up for crazy.

As we explored the city that weekend, we found ourselves craving more. We were unconsciously falling in love with New York, resonating with the determination and vulnerability in the faces all around us. After the final church service that evening, Gabe leaned in over late-night coffee and sheepishly asked if I would consider living in this place. His coy grin attempted to conceal his excitement, but the gleam in his eye gave him away. I knew as I answered that my exhilaration matched his.

The following months back in Atlanta led to countless hours surfing for apartment rentals and obscenely priced townhomes. But we would not be deterred. We could survive on rice and beans, if need be. As the anticipation grew, our silence gave way, and we confessed to our friends that we would move the following summer. There were many decisions to be made; yet the call to New York had grown so strong in both our hearts that running from the obstacles was not an option.

Restlessness continued to build. Some days I tried to blame the insanity of this leap on my husband, but I was also ready to jump. Something was tugging, pulling, screaming for me to make a dramatic alteration. In the end, I couldn't shake it. Something was calling, beckoning me into the unknown. Perhaps you've found yourself in a similar situation.

Describe the circumstances around a time when you have felt unsettled or restless.

When have you found yourself in a tug-of-war between two directions in your life?

When have you fought against God or held back in fear of the unknown?

I sensed life growing shorter by the minute in Atlanta, and I didn't want to live with regret. ... So, despite moments of kicking and screaming, I eventually surrendered. And once that decision was made, all the forces of providence moved in the direction of New York.

Yet what began as anticipation for this new adventure with God eventually was overtaken by tears of pain. I felt alone and uneasy. As if I were standing on the edge of the abyss of uncertainty. The tips of my toes hung over the cliff, and my body shifted forward. I was being thrust into my life's greatest freefall thus far, and I was leaving behind those who mattered most—my dearest friends. *Who will catch me?* I wondered to myself. *Who will catch me when I fall?* Perhaps these emotions aren't only mine.

Have you ever felt like you were falling into the great unknown? *yes*

Why are we so often afraid of the unknown future?

We are afraid of not having control over our circumstances

Not knowing what the future holds is a tough place. It is the great unknown where you know things could go many different ways—sometimes in your favor but other times not.

In that fear of the unknown we can relate to David in the Bible. King Saul had pursued David and was set on destroying him (see 1 Sam. 24). However, when David had his fair opportunity of killing King Saul in a cave, he chose to spare his life.

Saul was fair game. All David's men were ready to take the life of the king, yet David protected him. David did not know how Saul would respond when he confessed that he had cut the corner of Saul's robe—that David had had the opportunity to kill Saul. He did not know if Saul would turn on him and seek to kill him in that moment. Still in David's uncertainty, when his mind was telling him of the danger, David did what was right in God's eyes and acted in obedience to Him.

It is easy to read this when we have the full story and we see that everything turned out fine for David in the end. He didn't lose his life to Saul. He didn't live in hiding in a cave his entire life. However, in the moment with uncertainty looming, David knew what it was like to feel afraid for his life and for the unknown future that lay ahead. David cried out to God for help.

Have mercy on me, O God, have mercy!
I look to you for protection.
I will hide beneath the shadow of your wings
until the danger passes by.
I cry out to God Most High,
to God who will fulfill his purpose for me.
He will send help from heaven to rescue me,
disgracing those who hound me.
My God will send forth his unfailing love and faithfulness.

PSALM 57:1-3, NLT

In Psalm 57, David writes of his distress and praises
God for His protection. As you read Psalm 57:1-3,
what emotions did you sense in David?

fear and anxiety
trust in God's purpose

When David fled and hid from Saul in a cave, he prayed for God's mercy
and grace. David acknowledged that all his dependence was upon God and
that he took refuge in God alone. He humbly confessed his confidence in
God and trusted that his troubles would end well, that the danger would
pass. He confidently understood that he was under God's divine protection.

Even in this tough place, David saw the hand of God working for His
purposes. David's trust in God outweighed any fear or concerns for the
future or his life. David challenges us to lean into God, to "cry out to God
Most High" (v. 2), and to trust that He will fulfill His purposes for us. Every
single one of us.

I knew this move was something God had planned for us, but I had
reached a point where I was so afraid of what He had planned. However,
regret is when you know you should do something and choose not to, and
I didn't want to live with that.

Surrender

...

When we don't have an answer, we stay far from the ledge. Far from the possibility of failure or pain. Because falling without a safety net terrifies us.

This move to New York had beckoned me. How hard I resisted. But I wasn't fighting anymore. I was following it. Surrendering to it. Walking into it. Like David in Psalm 57, I faced an unknown, scary, irrational future. It was a midlife redirect with three children, two toy poodles, and a minivan—which isn't exactly cool anywhere, but definitely not in New York City.

From the South to the North.

From the suburbs to the city.

From margin to constraint.

Who will catch me? I wondered. My safety net severed, I descended into the unknown. But perhaps this was a gift in disguise.

After all, sometimes we need a freefall to teach us how to fly.

What does a freefall mean to you?

Who or what acts as your safety net?

What scares you the most about a freefall?

Perhaps a freefall for most of us means letting go. So we fight against anything that causes us to feel like control is out of our grasp. The Bible even lifts up self-control. Read from 2 Peter.

Supplement your faith with virtue, and virtue with knowledge, and knowledge with self-control, and self-control with steadfastness, and steadfastness with godliness, and godliness with brotherly affection, and brotherly affection with love. For if these qualities are yours and are increasing, they keep you from being ineffective or unfruitful in the knowledge of our Lord Jesus Christ.

2 PETER 1:5-8

Notice how the qualities listed in 2 Peter build upon each other:
Faith with virtue
  Virtue with knowledge
    Knowledge with self-control
      Self-control with steadfastness
        Steadfastness with godliness
          Godliness with brotherly affection
          Brotherly affection with love

What's the significance of self-control being listed in the middle of these qualities? What does that show about its importance?

Read from the Book of 2 Timothy.

> For people will be lovers of self, lovers of money, proud, arrogant, abusive, disobedient to their parents, ungrateful, unholy, heartless, unappeasable, slanderous, without self-control, brutal, not loving good, treacherous, reckless, swollen with conceit, lovers of pleasure rather than lovers of God, having the appearance of godliness, but denying its power.
>
> 2 TIMOTHY 3:2-5

List the negative qualities that Paul warns are associated with difficult times. What do you think is the significance of "without self-control" included in this list?

Self-control is applauded. Lack of self-control is seen as unfavorable and harmful. Our natural tendency is to desire a sense of control. However, for us to freefall it means letting go. We are asked to release control of ourselves to God and His plans instead of our own.

God calls us to control ourselves, to be patient, kind, and forgiving. Yet He also calls us to true faith in Him—to use self-control to solely focus ourselves on His plan and purposes. To allow Him to guide us down unknown paths, even when that means uncertainty and struggle.

Detoured

...

When we moved to Georgia after getting married, I grew comfortable in my skin. Our napkin dreams seemed to be materializing. Maybe we had both found our niches.

Then life happened.

Our first son, Cade—now the oldest of three—was born with Down syndrome. My doll baby. He never really cried. We played dress up, and he tolerated it with a gooey grin. But within months, his physical, speech, and occupational therapies increased to eight hours per week. I confessed to my boss that I was failing on both ends—as a team player and as a mom. I needed to dive deep into the role only I could fill. So home I went, to long days in a house swollen with silence.

God allows difficulties in our lives to direct us closer to His plan for us. But what are we supposed to do when we feel like God isn't there, when hope is fleeting?

Read Psalm 42. What specific verses in this psalm resonate with you and why?

Longing. It is obvious in this psalm that the writer has a deep longing for something more. The Hebrew verb *arag* implies that the subject pursues the Lord with a sense of urgency born of desperation and the knowledge that hope lies in no other. Often when we face distressing circumstances, antagonistic people, or a detour that completely alters what we thought God had planned, we feel this inner battle between despair and hope like the psalmist.

What situations or circumstances have put you on a detour that completely altered what you thought God had planned?

How did it feel to be downcast or in turmoil?

How did the situation change your hope for the future?

How do we handle life in the detour, the freefall, when everything seems completely out of control?

The afternoon before his first birthday, Cade napped as I methodically iced a huge lion face on a cake, made from scratch and complete with piped ribbons reflecting sugary oranges and browns.

Everything needs to be perfect. Look perfect. Taste perfect.

The same way I want Cade to be perfect.

My human attempt to find perfection. How was I still missing it? When would this pain subside? When would I shed the guilt I harbored for asking these questions and the crippling numbness when God didn't seem to answer?

I told a friend one day we were praying for Cade to be "whole." She responded, "Maybe your version of wholeness and God's version of wholeness look different." Reeling. *What does she know? She doesn't even have babies yet.*

A decade later. She was right.

My hang-up with wholeness was my issue, not Cade's. Not God's. In all the conversations during my first year as a mom, that is the only one I remember. But I wouldn't embrace it for years to come.

Perhaps that's why I kept notebooks chock full of to-do lists. Each item I added made me feel as though I had purpose. The longer the list, the greater the purpose. I became a rote, hollow version of my once-creative self. Success was measured by accomplishments each day. I went through mental gymnastics in bed each night, compulsively adding new things to my list. Tasking was my way of healing. But it was a lie. More like my distraction from grieving. My ability to keep things under control.

In my freefall, I was reminded that I didn't have control. I had stopped focusing on God's plans for my days—no matter how tiring and mundane they seemed at times. God had me firm in His grasp—and Proverbs reminds me that this includes my future.

> ### The heart of man plans his way, but the LORD establishes his steps.
>
> **PROVERBS 16:9**

We are responsible people. We like to think, to solve problems, to plan, and to look ahead to the future. Our hearts like to set a course and follow through, but unless the Lord directs our steps, our plans will fail.

> ### You do not know what tomorrow will bring. What is your life? For you are a mist that appears for a little time and then vanishes. Instead you ought to say, "If the Lord wills, we will live and do this or that."
>
> **JAMES 4:14-15**

What are some specific ways that you desperately try to keep control of your life?

God has constant control and care over our lives, even when we don't see or feel that way. Romans reminds us of this.

> # And we know that for those who love God all things work together for good, for those who are called according to his purpose.
>
> **ROMANS 8:28**

We read this verse, but do we really believe it? Do we really trust that God is working all things together for good? In the daily grind of working and parenting and relationship struggles, it can be hard to internalize. I was flailing between the many blessings I had been given and the dull ache of wanting something more.

As my fears of being a mediocre parent grew, I became delirious with exhaustion. I felt guilty for not loving the moments more. I grieved for not loving the messiness more. Try as I might, I could not manipulate those shining moments any more than I could pretend to cherish them.

Over time, the lists started losing their savor. They became less frequent. Days would sneak by without a glance. Tasking turned to turmoil. *Am I living the life I always imagined? Is this what the rest of my days are destined to look like? Will I always be forced to abandon hope for duty?*

If we ignore the yearnings of our souls, we atrophy, and our dreams die. Sadly, many of us choose this descent because we believe it's safer. If we don't hope, we won't be let down. If we don't imagine, reality won't disappoint. Either way, we avoid pain.

A friend recently confessed through tears that she struggles with bitterness. Her life doesn't look the way she'd hoped it would. She couldn't reconcile how her life—looking so successful on the surface—disguised the aching void that brings her tears the moment she opens her balled fists. *Are we grieving because our lives don't look the way we imagined in our youth? Do we pressure our children to reach their potential because we aren't living up to our own? Are we spending every moment cultivating the lives of everyone . . . but ourselves?*

We find ourselves unable to dream beyond our current reality. So we compromise. *My childhood dreams were just that—dreams. I should let them go.* We push down any hope when we sense it emerging. The desire for change uncovers what terrifies us most: failure.

What is it about failure that scares you most?

How might fear be holding you back from accomplishing something you've longed to achieve?

Read Psalm 115:11. How can this verse encourage you to let go of the fear? Of what God desires to do in your life?

How might your life change if you lean into the Lord more and trust Him for your good?

We tell ourselves a quick fix will do just fine. Whatever will keep our heads above water—whatever will allow us to keep making lunches, paying the bills, doing the kids' carpool, working out, pursuing that career, and so on—will just have to do. We don't want to become the crazy lady at the bus stop, so we think to ourselves, *Just give me the shortcut. Then I'll be okay.*

Perhaps most alarming are the many women who don't see past their manicured lives—grasping for society's definition of being "put together." We have pretty ways of masking our lack of meaning, using all kinds of beauty products and retail therapy. We have homes to furnish and decorate, then redecorate once we tire of what we have. We keep up with fashion styles, throw and attend parties, and maintain a rigorous pace. While these are all delightful and beautiful and often worthy goals, using them to conceal our unfulfilled lives is dangerous.

What do you use to mask your insecurities? Your fears? Your lack of trust in God?

We were each created to be fulfilled through our own unique purposes. Read from Psalm 139.

For you formed my inward parts; you knitted me together in my mother's womb. I praise you, for I am fearfully and wonderfully made. Wonderful are your works; my soul knows it very well. My frame was not hidden from you, when I was being made in secret, intricately woven in the depths of the earth. Your eyes saw my unformed substance; in your book were written, every one of them, the days that were formed for me, when as yet there was none of them.

PSALM 139:13-16

You were wonderfully created by an Almighty God. How does this impact the way you view yourself?

How do these verses impact the way you view your relationship with God?

It is difficult to be in a place in life where we are seeking purpose. What we don't realize is that this struggle is often a gift that leads us to a new place. A place with determination to be all that God created us to be.

The Bible is full of evidence that you were created with a purpose … with a story. Read the following verses.

> So God created man in his own image, in the image of God
> he created him; male and female he created them.
>
> GENESIS 1:27

> Everyone who is called by my name, whom I created
> for my glory, whom I formed and made.
>
> ISAIAH 43:7

> Before I formed you in the womb I knew you,
> and before you were born I consecrated you;
> I appointed you a prophet to the nations.
>
> JEREMIAH 1:5

What strikes you most about these verses?

As you learn to claim that you were created by a sovereign God with a purpose, it's time to start searching for what that looks like in your day-to-day life. Yes, life gets busy and messy and eventually you feel like giving up when things get too hard or you just want to "numb out" instead of deal with reality, but the answer to the following question should be a resounding, "YES!": Can a woman chase the dreams that stir her heart when life gets in the way?

Mission

Aging is paradoxical: the older you get, the less you are sure of. Perhaps you thought you had faith figured out before, when life was a negative in black and white. But now, as an adult, you see in full color, and the image has faded. So you're stuck in a freefall because you never figured out what makes you fly.

Why do you think women begin to push their dreams aside as life begins to happen?

What dreams have you put on hold?

Most of us have a desire to do something with our lives that leaves a lasting mark—something that makes a difference for our family, friends, and others in the world. But most of us don't even know how to put it into words. Try right now.

What does that desire feel like or look like to you?

It's so important that we understand God has planned good works for us to accomplish through Him.

For we are his workmanship, created in Christ Jesus for good works, which God prepared beforehand, that we should walk in them.

EPHESIANS 2:10

Is it a relief that you only need to seek God to find what He has planned, or would you rather everything be up to you? Explain.

At first glance, what are some of your current routines that reflect a life well spent?

What are some of your current routines that you use as an "exhale" or to "numb out" when you feel directionless at your core?

What ideas, things, or habits will you need to let go of in order to begin your freefall—to really trust that God has your best interest at heart?

Spend some time talking to or writing to God about this process. What do you hope to experience and learn? Ask Him to make His presence known to you—to wrap His arms around you as you trust Him. Relish the anticipation of eventually learning to fly.

Tweet what you're learning: #freefalltofly

Journal

These pages are for you to make your own. One of the many great benefits of journaling our thoughts and the details of our lives is that we have a safe place to spill out all of the confusion brewing inside and mingle it with the thankfulness and hope that keeps us afloat. It gives us a place to come back to at some point in the future to see how far we've come.

CHAPTER 2

...

Freefall

Our own attempts have failed us.
The life we have orchestrated falls
flat and leaves us lying in a corner,
huddled in despair in those dark
hours of the early morning.

If you cling to your life, you will lose it; but if you
give up your life for me, you will find it.
MATTHEW 10:39, NLT

For me, doing the actual work to fulfill the vision is the
easy part. It's the emotional journey that I go through as
I am free falling into the unknown that is the hard part.
But each time I jump, I'm learning to trust that God will
continue to guide me and help me to land safely.
YVONNE PIERRE, *THE DAY MY SOUL CRIED*[1]

#

···

adapted excerpts from chapter 2 of Freefall to Fly

I resolved to make a go of my new life. Rather than allow my children to shrink their brain mass in front of the television screen, I began scheming ways to breathe life into their afternoons.

Scouring the Internet for free, kid-friendly activities, I stumbled across the Mommy Poppins website. Sweet relief. Someone brilliant had gone before me and paved the way for doing life in the city, kids in tow. I scribbled a list of the best options and, at the finish, admired the collection. Creative. Educational. We might just have a chance at this.

I called it Camp Mom, and for a few days it provided a sense of purpose I'd not felt since we moved. Each day, my children would follow me down the street like ducklings ready to embark on a new adventure. Art history classes at the Met. Rock climbing at Chelsea Piers. Mini–roller coasters in Central Park. Live sea lion feedings at the zoo. Book readings at the public library.

I was beginning to settle in when the heat swooped in.

Mommy Poppins revealed a public pool not far from our townhome. It overlooked the East River near Carl Schurz Park. How charming.

Donning sunscreen and grabbing water bottles, we plodded (Cade's new NYC pace) to First Avenue and waited fifteen minutes for the city bus to arrive while Cade, despite my pleas, lay on the filthy dog-pee-covered curb. The bus stopped every two blocks for the next thirty minutes until we arrived at East 87th. We trudged yet another two avenues toward the river, adding up to a full forty-five minutes of commitment, before I spotted the rectangular, concrete water hole on the horizon. Quiet. Clear. Awaiting our arrival.

We walked through several sets of iron gates before arriving at the locker room entrance. A security guard stood at the opening with a scowl on her face. Perhaps she was armed. I didn't want to find out.

"Where's your lock?" she barked.

"What lock?"

"The padlock for your locker."

"I don't have one. I didn't see anything like that on the website."

"I don't know nothing about a website, but you need a lock."

"I'm so sorry—we don't have anything valuable. Can we please just leave our things in the locker?"

"Nope." She stepped in front of the doorway, and I panicked.

"Please. My children and I traveled forty-five minutes to get here, and no one is even in the pool right now. Could we just stay for a few minutes?"

"Nope."

Her stone face served as one more reminder that we weren't in the suburbs anymore. Not exactly what I needed at that moment.

Then the questions began.

The questions you have no energy to answer. Because, quite frankly, you don't have an answer. And even if you tried to muster the logic required to make this a teaching moment for your children, you don't have the stamina. Sweaty and smelly, I stared at a bird flitting around the park. I envied her.

My son Pierce began cautiously: "Why do we need to have a lock?"

Silence.

He paused and tried again.

"It's silly to bring a lock to a swimming pool, isn't it, Mom?"

I was neither able nor willing to transform this into a teaching moment. No lesson existed, and I was almost too angry to speak. I'd been using Camp Mom to distract me from my own unhappiness, and our first run-in with misfortune was forcing me to confront my emotions once more.

I snapped.

"I hate New York, and you can tell your father I said that," I said to Pierce.

"You don't really mean that, do you, Mom?"

"Yes. Yes, I do."

And with those words hanging in the stale afternoon air, I phoned my husband. I'm not sure what I said in that moment, but I know the words weren't kind, and I remember demanding that he arrive within twenty minutes with a lock or I'd come unglued. Or worse.

Usually our breaking points happen over something that might seem small or insignificant to someone else (you call THAT a problem?), but those moments highlight something much deeper that has been stirring and waiting to bubble to the surface.

Have you experienced a "Camp Mom" type moment recently? What were the circumstances?

How did you vent your frustrations?

The heaviness lifted until bedtime, when I overheard Pierce in his bed talking to his dad. Uh-oh. Is he going to make good on my demands?

"Mommy wants me to tell you she hates New York. Do you think she really means that?"

"No, Son, I think she was just frustrated. It's okay."

Busted.

Gabe entered to find my face buried in a pillow: "Honey, you really should edit your words in front of the kids."

Ashamed.

I'd self-destructed again. Pinned in a corner on a park bench, I'd lashed out against Gabe and against this city, using my son as a pawn in my scheme. The failure had overwhelmed me. And the rejection. And the helplessness. Here I was, giving my everything to Camp Mom, but the effort wasn't bringing true happiness. Shunned to a park bench with my kids, on the outside looking in. Pinned in a corner, not getting my way. ...

I was awakening to a truth: desperation often leads to self-destruction. When hope is lost, we start doing things we wouldn't normally do. Lashing out where the cost is greatest. We begin to destroy ourselves and go after the people we love most. Because we assume they are indestructible. That they will never break. Never leave. Never walk away.

Because they are ours.

Because they love us.

Because we can.

Desperation often leads to self-destruction. When hope is lost, we start doing things we wouldn't normally do. Lashing out where the cost is greatest.

What is your defense mechanism when you feel desperate?

Who has been hurt along the way when you've lashed out or started to self-destruct in a stressful situation?

Let's face it. It's easy to become absorbed in our struggles. At times, it even can be overwhelming. Granted, my moment of breakdown outside the pool wasn't because of horrible circumstances or events, yet it was a clear warning sign that I wasn't focusing on the right things. Read what James has to say about facing difficulty.

> Count it all joy, my brothers, when you meet trials of various kinds, for you know that the testing of your faith produces steadfastness. And let steadfastness have its full effect, that you may be perfect and complete, lacking in nothing.
>
> JAMES 1:2-4

Notice this passage says "*when* you meet trials." Difficulty. Hardship. Pain. Heartache. It's all a part of life. We are going to struggle. Yet if we focus on the remainder of those verses, we see that something good can come from the bad. God is using those struggles to bring about our perfection. Completeness. Wholeness in Him.

Name one major trial you've faced and overcome. How did God help you through it? What good has come of that struggle?

Read James 1:12. What things can you do to remain "steadfast under trial"?

Pause

...

My tears crashed on my pillowcase with the full comprehension of all my limitations. Limitations of the mundane that used to come so easily. This city would push me to get on my knees, to grovel, to fully enter into my weakness. In my cries of lament, I heard a word so clearly it almost sounded audible: *Stay.*

"What does that even mean?"

Stay in the freefall.

A truth hit me in that moment. *All my life, I've been running.* Running to the next greatest thing. An adventurer. A thrill seeker. Hungry for more. If things got hard, *fight or flight.* I would kick and scream for a while, and when that didn't yield the proper results, I would take flight. It happened in my closest relationships. Including my arguments with Gabe. If I was not able to win or be understood, I'd grow silent and escape. Far away. To a place that allowed me to maintain control. But the silent treatment and hibernation never brought relief; instead, I felt abandoned by my own doing. All alone. By my own choosing. This defense of self-preservation left me on the altar of self-destruction.

But now what I was hearing for the first time was that the fear of entrapment was running right along with me. Following me. Chasing me. Changing my circumstances wouldn't give me reprieve, just a new setting.

To stay in the freefall meant to stop running. To stop avoiding the pain. To embrace the struggle. To settle in with the lament. To get cozy with my nemesis. Because it was working something out in me that was buried deep. Locked down for a number of years. Wounds that had been planted long ago were starting to show their ugly heads. I was scared. But I needed to give them room to surface. To let them out.

As we experience our rapid descents, how many of us reach out for anything we can grab to break our fall? To escape the pain. To find a way to numb out. We don't believe God will actually rescue, so we sidestep. We look for a shortcut. Any way out. Because it hurts too much, and it has gone on for far too long. We are weary. Frankly, we are angry that it has gotten this hard. We've complained so long, even we are sick of hearing ourselves, never mind the effect it's having on those around us.

How do you typically spend your time waiting for something to be resolved? Do you keep trying to find ways to maintain control? Do you numb out or hide out? Do you run? Or do you use it as a time of reflection and growth?

Why might a loving God ask you or someone you love to stay in a painful situation for longer than you had hoped?

What things about God, His character, and His discipline might He want you to learn? Make notes as you read through the following verses.

☐ Proverbs 3:1-6

☐ Proverbs 12:1-3

☐ Hebrews 12:1-11

God, in His omniscience, knows us to our core. He understands our pain. He sees our weaknesses. And He loves us anyway. There is nowhere we can run to escape His presence. What's more, He longs to bring light to our darkness.

Where shall I go from your Spirit?
Or where shall I flee from your presence?
If I ascend to heaven, you are there!
If I make my bed in Sheol, you are there!
If I take the wings of the morning
and dwell in the uttermost parts of the sea,
even there your hand shall lead me,
and your right hand shall hold me.
11 If I say, "Surely the darkness shall cover me,
and the light about me be night,"
even the darkness is not dark to you;
the night is bright as the day,
for darkness is as light with you.

PSALM 139:7-12

According to these verses, there is nowhere we can go that God cannot find us. Does this bring you relief or frustration? Why?

Even when you try to hide in darkness or flee, verse 10 says that God's hand will hold you and lead you. What is keeping you from allowing Him to do this?

Why is it that we struggle to fully trust our very Creator and Sustainer? Waiting on and seeking God is the very expression of having faith in Him. It's trusting that when we encounter difficulty—when we're hanging on by a thread and don't know what to do next—He is there. Watching over us. Loving us, despite our faults. Guiding our steps.

Have you not known? Have you not heard?
The LORD is the everlasting God,
the Creator of the ends of the earth.
He does not faint or grow weary;
his understanding is unsearchable.
He gives power to the faint,
and to him who has no might he increases strength.
Even youths shall faint and be weary,
and young men shall fall exhausted;
but they who wait for the LORD shall renew their strength;
they shall mount up with wings like eagles;
they shall run and not be weary;
they shall walk and not faint.

ISAIAH 40:28-31

According to these verses, what is the benefit of waiting on and trusting in the Lord?

When life is heavy and hard to take, go off by yourself. Enter the silence. Bow in prayer. Don't ask questions: Wait for hope to appear. Don't run from trouble. Take it full-face. The "worst" is never the worst.

> GOD proves to be good to the man who passionately waits, to the woman who diligently seeks. It's a good thing to quietly hope, quietly hope for help from GOD. It's a good thing when you're young to stick it out through the hard times.
>
> **LAMENTATIONS 3:25-26, MSG**

What truths from this passage did you need to hear today in your current situation(s)?

The Bible is full of examples from those who had to wait during difficult times. Joseph remained faithful to God after encountering much hardship and imprisonment. He was later promoted to governor of Egypt because of his interpretation of Pharaoh's dream (see Gen. 37–50). Hannah was unable to conceive, and yet continued to plead with God. After years of being shamed by her community, she gave birth to a son, Samuel, who would later be named in the "hall of faith" (see 1 Sam. 1:9-28; Heb. 11). Esther, Ruth, Abraham and Sarah, Zechariah and Elizabeth, Job, Moses, Paul, and Jesus Himself—the list is endless of those who have shown us that we need to faithfully wait on God's timing.

I believe that I shall look upon the goodness of the LORD
in the land of the living!
Wait for the LORD;
be strong, and let your heart take courage;
wait for the LORD!

PSALM 27:13-14

Therefore the LORD waits to be gracious to you,
and therefore he exalts himself to show mercy to you.
For the LORD is a God of justice;
blessed are all those who wait for him.

ISAIAH 30:18

What does waiting on the Lord look like in your current context?

Look back at the verses you've read today. Which ones give you hope? Write them on index cards and stick them somewhere that you will read them often. Repetition will ingrain the promises in your heart and mind.

Growth
...

In life, we are often the authors of our own tragedies. Sure, we blame those around us. Our parents. Our teachers. Those who've hurt us. But we sit at a metaphorical writer's desk, scribbling and scratching out many of our lives' details. Our own hands often insert a little mishap here. A small mistake there. Though we'd like to blame any misfortune on our ethereal "circum-stances," we've been penning the plot in this tragedy the whole time.

Gabe called my bluff. My marriage was becoming a game of tug-of-war. Camp Mom had not left me fulfilled, and my children were sensing the tangled ball of yarn that was my emotional state. And Gabe wasn't going to let me pass the blame. I apologized, more embarrassed about being called out than repentant. Of course Pierce—that fragile young vine—couldn't stop a freefall. So I left him in my wake and sadly continued my downward descent.

Think about something from your past that has caused you the greatest amount of pain, shame, or embarrassment. Write about it here in as much detail as you can bear.

Is there someone besides yourself whom you blame for this pain? Write out what you would want to say to them. Then spend as much time as you need to pray and ask God to help you forgive that person so you can truly heal.

Now, take responsibility for your part in this pain. What can you personally do right now to turn things around and make things better? What steps do you need to take?

We've been talking of this concept of a freefall—this process of willingly letting go and falling into the capable arms of God. Think about what it would be like to fall into the arms of your Creator who is waiting to catch you. What would that be like?

In the space provided, draw a picture or write a story of what you just pondered. Include words or drawings that represent those things He is going to take from you (fear, control, etc.).

Somewhere along the way, if you stay in the place where your heart breaks and you put one foot in front of the other, the darkness will eventually lift. The crack of light will burst forth on the horizon, far, far away. It will be the slightest breath of hope. Just like the word *stay* was for me. You won't know what that light will yield, but the mere fact that it is light will be enough.

It will keep you going. Embrace the fall. Have faith that God is there to catch you.

Tweet what you're learning: *#freefalltofly*

Journal

CHAPTER 3

...

Naming Fears

We can't choose to surrender. It chooses
us. It finds us and meets us in our
pain. When we are at our lowest point.
In our weariness. In our longing.

Don't be afraid, for I am with you. Don't be discouraged,
for I am your God. I will strengthen you and help you.
I will hold you up with my victorious right hand.
ISAIAH 41:10, NLT

Leave the Irreparable Past in His hands, and step
out into the Irresistible Future with Him.
OSWALD CHAMBERS,
MY UTMOST FOR HIS HIGHEST[1]

Panic

...

adapted excerpts from Chapter 3 of Freefall to Fly

I boarded the plane and dove headfirst into a new book, given to me by a dear friend the day prior. I uncovered the author's observation that we as women pretend we don't need anything. We carry the load and often ask for nothing in return. Those of us who are full-time mothers manage our homes, nurse our babies, tutor our children, become chefs and expert organizers, and along the way support our husbands (if they're still around). Many mothers also work full-time, providing financial support or perhaps the only income.

No matter our circumstances, there seems little room for women to have their own dreams.

With these realizations fresh in my mind, I stumbled upon this:

> "Our deepest fear is not that we are inadequate. Our deepest fear is that we are powerful beyond measure. It is our light, not our darkness that most frightens us." We ask ourselves, Who am I to be brilliant, gorgeous, talented, fabulous? Actually, who are you *not* to be? You are a child of God. Your playing small does not serve the world. . . . We were born to make manifest the glory of God that is within us. And as we let our own light shine, we unconsciously give other people permission to do the same.[2]

Finally I was able to name the fear I had carried for so long: I would never be worthy of the purpose God might have for me, even though I knew in my mind that wasn't true.

So I avoided anything that pushed me in that direction, because it was unknown and I was uncertain. But here I was, awakening to this urging again. Naming it. Feeling it. Breaking under it. Perhaps God did have something for me. If only I would walk into it.

For I know the plans I have for you, declares the LORD, plans for welfare and not for evil, to give you a future and a hope. Then you will call upon me and come and pray to me, and I will hear you. You will seek me and find me, when you seek me with all your heart.

JEREMIAH 29:11-13

When has fear so gripped you that you held back despite knowing God has a purpose for you?

How have you avoided responsibilities or direction from God?

In what seemed like minutes, the plane began its descent. Suddenly the cabin began to rock. Then shake. And then turbulence took over and tossed passengers around like rag dolls. Stomachs heaving. Fingers clenched. Something took over inside me. I could not stop the gripping fear that encompassed me. I had the uncontrollable urge to get up, yell out, and run to the front, all while trying to keep my heart contained.

Suspended in the stratosphere, I was having a full-blown panic attack.

The moment the plane's wheels met the asphalt, I sprang up and ran from seat 29B—three rows from the back—all the way to the front galley of the plane while it was still careening to a halt down the runway. The flight attendant looked up in horror as she saw me barreling toward her. I collapsed to my knees in front of her and pressed my head into the aisle floor, choking out these words:

"Panic . . . attack."

I'm thankful that flight attendants see these occurrences often and that captains do, too. The copilot came out from the cockpit to reassure and comfort me.

Afterward, I endured my walk of shame. It involved little walking, actually. I sat in the front row of seats waiting for every last person to exit. Though my eyes remained fixed on the carpet, with every passing pair of feet I could feel a concerned stare for the pitiful girl who had lost her mind.

The weeks that followed became a downward spiral of panic attacks. Inhale, exhale.

I was now crippled.

Fear was taking over. Something inside me was dying. Each encounter, however brief, was stealing from me. My freedom, my independence, and most of all, my control. I was losing faith in my ability to conquer the terror.

The anxiety reached a crescendo on Thanksgiving Day. How I wish I had anticipated this scenario. We were hosting three families in our Upper East Side apartment that afternoon with turkey and all the fixin's. But first we were taking the kids to the Macy's Thanksgiving Day Parade. Imagine if the New Year's Eve Times Square masses relocated along the border of Central Park. You get the picture.

The veteran Macy's paraders were not going to let me and my three tykes push through to Daddy. Cell service was gone. The crowds even suppressed text messages. I had no way to communicate as I helplessly stood two hundred feet away. Finally my call to Gabe went through, and my frantic voice screamed above the noise, "I can't do it! If you want the kids to see this, you will have to come get them!"

Tears fell as my kids bore witness to my weakness once more. I didn't have what it took to push through. Not the strength, ability, or will.

Who was I becoming? The Rebekah I once knew was fearless and aggressive. Demanding, even rude, if need be. She was capable and strong. A mob was no match for her. But I couldn't find her.

The fear of losing one of my kids in that ferocious crowd had just been too much. What if Cade had decided he wasn't in the mood? Or Pierce and Kennedy had gotten separated or lost? Worse yet, what if we'd gotten halfway into the crowd and I couldn't take another step? The fears were real.

I remembered the freedom I had felt after my bedside commitment to stop the running. However, *recognizing* my need wasn't enough. Staying in the freefall was getting harder. The descent faster. Would someone really catch me? I feared there would be no one at the bottom.

A famous line counselors use is "The first step to recovery is to admit there is a problem." But what was the second step? We can stop fleeing, but eventually we must turn around and stare our brokenness in the face. Deal with the ugliness we've fled for so long. I knew I needed to turn around. To confront my anxiety. My fear. My unhappiness.

In order to face our fears, struggles, and woundings, we have to name them. We can't give up something if we can't identify it.

Take time now to start naming your fears. What causes you to grip the arm rest? To fall on your knees breathless? To run in the opposite direction? To pretend it doesn't exist?

Scripture reminds us again and again of people who have faced their fears head-on and overcome them with God's strength.

Read each passage from Genesis below. Write in the fears of each person and how each was resolved.

Person	Scripture	Fear	Resolution
Abram	Genesis 15		
Lot	Genesis 19:30		
Jacob	Genesis 32:11		
Joseph's brothers	Genesis 43–50		

Who else from Scripture can you name that overcame fears?

Some of our struggles, like the example in the earlier Marianne Williamson quote, are difficult to name, but in examples like mine, there are words that come to mind: Anxiety. Depression. Insignificance. Loneliness. Failure. The fear of someone you love getting hurt or dying. The fear of not being able to provide. Anxiety for the future. Name them, sisters!

Now fill in the following chart of your own fears, struggles, and woundings.

Name your fears.   **What did you miss out on in life because of them?**

_____

_____

_____

_____

_____

_____

_____

_____

Could it be that the aching we tried to describe earlier is there because we are missing out on the lives we were meant to live? Could it be that fears and past wounds have held us captive for so long we don't know how to let go and move forward?

Depending on which version of the Bible you are using, phrases such as "do not fear," "do not let your heart be troubled," and "do not be afraid" appear almost 300 times. God should only have to mention it once for us to obey it, but knowing our fleshly tendencies, He kept saying it over and over. He means what He says.

Take a moment to read through the following verses and allow God to speak to your particular situation.

Fear not, for I am with you;
be not dismayed, for I am your God;
I will strengthen you, I will help you,
I will uphold you with my righteous right hand.

ISAIAH 41:10

Peace I leave with you; my peace I give to you.
Not as the world gives do I give to you. Let not your
hearts be troubled, neither let them be afraid.

JOHN 14:27

Don't worry about anything; instead, pray
about everything. Tell God what you need,
and thank him for all he has done.

PHILIPPIANS 4:6, NLT

Give all your worries and cares to
God, for he cares about you.

1 PETER 5:7, NLT

What changes will need to take place in your life for
you to believe fully the truths found in these verses?

What will you need to give up?

In Revelation 21:8, "the fearful" (KJV) are included in a list with murderers,
idolaters, and liars of those who will "have their part in the lake which
burneth with fire and brimstone." There is no place for your fears. God's
truth trumps them all. Allow God's grace and power to overtake your fears
as you work to identify and release each one.

Obey

The quiet settled into the recesses of our old apartment as I recounted all that had transpired since that fateful day on the plane. I still couldn't shake the panic attack on that traumatic flight and what it had begun in me these past few weeks. Then I came across this quotation from Leo Tolstoy:

> The changes in our life must come from the impossibility to live otherwise than according to the demands of our conscience, not from our mental resolution to try a new form of life.[3]

My eyes widened with realization. I had made New York my mental resolution upon arrival. Willing my way through Camp Mom. Breaking down outside the public pool. Dragging Cade across Park Avenue. Weaving through the crowds at the Macy's Thanksgiving Day Parade. All with the intention of "a new form of life." I was trying everything in my power to find a life of meaning.

But wait. What was my conscience demanding? A conscience borne from the Creator. Jesus didn't mince words on this:

If you cling to your life, you will lose it; but if you give up your life for me, you will find it.

MATTHEW 10:39, NLT

In order to truly live, something would have to die to myself. With no idea where this breathtaking journey was going, I was on it—like it or not. But what would death look like for me?

Maybe you've been asking yourself the same questions.

Read Matthew 10:39 again. What does this verse mean to you?

What in you will need to die in order for you to live your life for Jesus without being bound by the things that hold you back?

We all have our own ideas about what we think our lives should look like, but anytime we're choosing our ways over God's ways we are living in disobedience. This disobedience is called "sin" in God's Word and it means "separation from God."

> But your iniquities have separated you from
> your God; your sins have hidden his face
> from you, so that he will not hear.
>
> ISAIAH 59:2, NIV

So, why does sin separate and why will God not hear us? The first part of Romans 6:23 says: "For the wages of sin is death." Our Holy God cannot be in the presence of sin and death, so when we've chosen a life of sin, we are not in a life-giving relationship with the One who gives life. We cannot live under the benefits of abiding in *His presence* if sin has created a chasm.

Thankfully, God does not leave us in our sin and death. He provided a way through the sacrifice of His only Son, Jesus. God's love for you is so deep that He allowed His Son to become the punishment for your sin.

> For God so loved the world that he gave his one
> and only Son, that whoever believes in him
> shall not perish but have eternal life.
>
> JOHN 3:16, NIV

So, how can we be rescued?

> If you confess with your mouth that Jesus is
> Lord and believe in your heart that God raised
> him from the dead, you will be saved.
>
> ROMANS 10:9

> For the wages of sin is death, but the free gift of
> God is eternal life in Christ Jesus our Lord.
>
> ROMANS 6:23

Perhaps you have read these verses a million times. Or maybe you are reading them for the first time and wondering what it all means. No matter your familiarity, we each serve the same loving God who wants us to be in a right-standing relationship with Him. Even if you are a "good" person, God needs all of you in complete surrender in order to use you. In order to show you what He has for you.

Read the following passage as a prayer to God and then spend time revisiting the question below it.

> Search me, O God, and know my heart!
> Try me and know my thoughts!
> And see if there be any grievous way in me,
> and lead me in the way everlasting!
>
> PSALM 139:23-24

What needs to change in your heart so that you might live for Christ? In your thoughts?

David realized that God thoroughly searched him. God misses nothing—no seemingly insignificant details, no cherished sin, no hidden agendas or motives, no unconscious memories or fears escape His notice. Though the Lord may seem far away because He is invisible to earthly eyes, He also perceives the thoughts that are inaccessible to others. David's response to the reality that God knows all was not of fear but of faith.

Confess to God the things that you know grieve Him. Remember sin is anything that separates you from God. Write down the sins that hold you back from Him and hinder you from being fully devoted to Him. Write down the selfish actions and attitudes that keep you from living in complete obedience to Him. Confess the unbelief or distrust you may have toward God. Don't hold back in fear of God, but instead respond in faith knowing He alone can change your heart, your mind, and transform your life.

Trust

...

Just thinking about changing your heart, mind, and living for Christ can be overwhelming at times. Our natural tendency is to panic when we think about releasing control. Pressure, anxiety, and worries are part of our culture. We cling to them like we cling to our control. At the root is our lack of trust. People have let us down so we expect them to let us down again. And somehow in our distrust for people we have a lack of trust in God. However, if we can move beyond the anxiety and worries that come with our lack of trust and make the decision to trust God, we will freefall—but then we will fly.

What would it take for you to truly trust God—to let go of your own plans—and freefall into His arms?

What does it take for us to have trust in someone or something?

God wants to remind you that you are loved. Read these verses and take note of what they say about God's love for you.

Blessed be the God and Father of our Lord Jesus Christ, who has blessed us in Christ with every spiritual blessing in the heavenly places, even as he chose us in him before the foundation of the world, that we should be holy and blameless before him. In love he predestined us for adoption as sons through Jesus Christ, according to the purpose of his will, to the praise of his glorious grace, with which he has blessed us in the Beloved.

EPHESIANS 1:3-6

See what kind of love the Father has given to us, that we should be called children of God; and so we are. The reason why the world does not know us is that it did not know him.

1 JOHN 3:1

In this the love of God was made manifest among us, that God sent his only Son into the world, so that we might live through him. In this is love, not that we have loved God but that he loved us and sent his Son to be the propitiation for our sins.

1 JOHN 4:9-10

How does it feel when you are reminded how much God loves you?

Christ laid down His life for us (see 1 John 3:16; 4:10) and love is from God (see 1 John 4:1,10). Because God loved us first (see 1 John 3:1; 4:19) we can love God in return and love others (see 1 John 3:23; 4:21; 5:2). Sometimes our struggles and circumstances may cause us to question God's love for us, but Scripture reminds us again and again that we can trust His love.

What's holding you back from trusting God?

What do you still need to release to Him?

Name those fears that keep you from trusting God completely. Commit to pray about each one daily asking God to guide you to a greater trust in Him.

Tweet what you're learning: #freefalltofly

_____

_____

_____

_____

_____

_____

_____

_____

_____

_____

_____

_____

_____

_____

_____

_____

_____

_____

_____

_____

_____

_____

_____

_____

_____

_____

_____

_____

_____

_____

CHAPTER 4

····

Surrender & Rescue

Surrender changes everything. ... It enters in when we have run out of our own strength. When we start to believe that things may never actually change. That our lives don't really matter ... and we break. Then we see it. The crack of sunrise. Just a glow on the horizon. Pink and orange starting to rise and create a hue that colors the sky.

He reached down from heaven and rescued me; he drew me out of deep waters. He rescued me from my powerful enemies, from those who hated me and were too strong for me. He led me to a place of safety; he rescued me because he delights in me.
PSALM 18:16-17,19, NLT

It is not trying that is ever going to bring us home. All this trying leads up to the vital moment at which you turn to God and say, "You must do this. I can't."
C.S. LEWIS[1]

Mend

adapted excerpts from Chapters 7 and 8 of Freefall to Fly

Take a moment to watch the video, "Being Made New," by author Rebekah Lyons, available for free at *www.lifeway.com/freefall.*

In the last chapter, you spent time naming fears, struggles, and past wounds. You faced them and brought them into the light. You learned that sometimes something has to die in order for you to live the life you were created to live. Then, you asked God to search your heart and to reveal anything that might be keeping you from having a life-giving relationship with Him.

When we pick up on my story, I had recently fallen fully back into a world of almost daily panic attacks. They were stealing my life, stealing my hope, and keeping me from moving forward.

Describe a time when you thought you were moving forward, only to relapse back into a previous struggle. Describe the feeling of defeat and what you did to survive.

The date was Tuesday, September 20. Otherwise a normal day. Gabe went to the office, and I headed across the park for another Tuesday morning with friends, hoping to conceal my troubles. As good girlfriends do, they asked me how I was doing. I shrugged and cried, again.

Without prompting, they surrounded me and prayed bold prayers. Long and loud. My hope was depleted. I was lost and confused. Yet this community of women believed in me. No, they believed *for* me. Their strength lifted me when I couldn't trust on my own.

Before bed that night, I lay on my back with my feet raised high against a wall. (Breathing exercises had become a part of my normal routine.) Soon after, I swallowed the little blue sleep aid and drifted off to sleep.

Awakened, again.

3:02 a.m.

I clutched Gabe's arm, squeezing and clasping. We both sat up straight in a silent impulse. I had no words. The air I tried so desperately to grasp seemed destined to stay away from my lungs. I struggled for speech, but nothing came.

He prayed, "God, take this panic away. You are not a God who invokes fear, but faith. Give us faith. Help Rebekah to breathe, to calm, to release."

Still no words. Just clutching at Gabe's bicep over and over and over. He kept praying. With all the will I could gather, I lifted my right hand and prayed in desperation, "God, rescue me! I can't do this without You!"

Then it happened. My body collapsed. I fell flat on the bed. Body still. No pounding, no trembling, just stillness. Something broke.

The physical bondage that I'd been battling for more than a year was gone in an instant. I had never come out of a panic attack like that before. I'd always had to escape my setting for it to subside. This was different. No running, just silence.

I mustered a whisper to Gabe: "Did you feel that?"

His questioning response: "You stopped?"

Tranquility. Falling into the arms of Something bigger, Someone stronger. The levity of a burden removed. As light as a bird with not a care in the world. More than just being heard, I was met in the moment. Carried by Him who knows all things. Speechless, I drifted back off to sleep.

I don't pretend to know the ways of God. When or how He chooses to liberate us.

For me, rescue came in my darkest hour. The moment I laid down the belief that I couldn't actually change. The instant I came to the end of myself and admitted defeat. In my final moment of surrender. I remembered the frightful words I'd underlined in a book during that fateful flight a year prior: *Death, a life-giving surrender. Rescue had come in my death.*

The night of my liberation, I experienced a physical breaking of the chains of fear I had been carrying for as long as I remembered.

> **How would your life or the life of someone you love look differently if rescue came right here, right now? Be as descriptive as possible.**

God's grace is always there. He is "the author and perfecter of faith"—not us (Heb. 12:2, NASB). We have to call out to Him and ask for His help, even in our unbelief. If we ask, He will strengthen us and help us fight against those things and people who are trying to steal our lives from us. He will draw near, but we need to ask.

God will always work everything out in His own timing. Even though He knows what we're going to say before we say it, He wants us to ask. He also asks us to intercede for others in order for His glory to be shown in a situation.

Spend a few moments reading through and processing the following verses. Allow God's Word to speak to your situation.

I will bless the LORD who guides me;
even at night my heart instructs me.
I know the LORD is always with me.
I will not be shaken, for he is right beside me.

PSALM 16:7-8, NLT

O LORD, you have examined my heart
and know everything about me.
You know when I sit down or stand up.
You know my thoughts even when I'm far away.
You see me when I travel
and when I rest at home.
You know everything I do.
You know what I am going to say
even before I say it, LORD.
You go before me and follow me.
You place your hand of blessing on my head.
Such knowledge is too wonderful for me,
too great for me to understand!
I could ask the darkness to hide me
and the light around me to become night—
but even in darkness I cannot hide from you.
You saw me before I was born.
Every day of my life was recorded in your book.
Every moment was laid out
before a single day had passed.

PSALM 139:1-6,11-12,16, NLT

Do you ever feel like you're just drifting through life? Do you wonder where your life is headed and what you've accomplished? Do you feel stuck on a treadmill of the mundane, working hard but not getting anywhere?

Most of us feel that way at some time or another. Those reflective thoughts reveal that God is calling you to Him, to focus you on what He has in store next. Just as Psalm 139 says, God knows you. He knows where you are headed, and He's going before you to draw you to His plan. God wants you to acknowledge your weakness, to seek Him and ask for His help. He will meet you there.

And this is the confidence that we have toward him, that if we ask anything according to his will he hears us.

1 JOHN 5:14

And so I tell you, keep on asking, and you will receive what you ask for. Keep on seeking, and you will find. Keep on knocking, and the door will be opened to you. For everyone who asks, receives. Everyone who seeks, finds. And to everyone who knocks, the door will be opened.

LUKE 11:9-10, NLT

What do these verses tell you about God's ability to transform you, even in the most hopeless situations?

The point isn't that God would grant anything we ask for. The point is surrendering ourselves so that eventually our desires would become that which God has planned for us. We must remain in Him and allow Him to transform our hearts.

But if you remain in me and my words remain in you, you may ask for anything you want, and it will be granted! When you produce much fruit, you are my true disciples. This brings great glory to my Father.

JOHN 15:7-8, NLT

When our panic sets in and we usher up prayers, desperate enough to jump off the seawall to swim for our lives, He rushes in with an overwhelming response. If only we would make that final call. It's the one action no one can do for us.

Jesus said, "Come to me, all of you who are weary and carry heavy burdens, and I will give you rest. Take my yoke upon you. Let me teach you, because I am humble and gentle at heart, and you will find rest for your souls. For my yoke is easy to bear, and the burden I give you is light."

MATTHEW 11:28-30, NLT

What seems unobtainable for the future? Write a prayer to God, asking for His help.

He promises our weary souls rest, but do we really believe Him? Do we trust that the God of this universe is strong enough to lighten our loads?

I wanted to believe it was possible, but for whatever reason, I couldn't until I had emptied myself, recognizing that I needed help.

I thought of my journey leading up to that night of deliverance. How long had I been carrying this burden, growing weaker by the day? Beaten down, treading a darkened path, weighed down with despair. I thought of so many of the beautiful women around me. Those who were heaving loads of stress and anxiety, piling on more and more burdens by the day.

But that night marked something different. I'd called for His help by choice, and He heard my cry.

In my distress I prayed to the LORD, and the LORD answered me and set me free.

PSALM 118:5, NLT

What a relief to know that God not only exists but also listens. He hears when we cry. And when He hears, He responds by liberating us. When I could do little more than lift my hands and exhale a desperate cry for rescue, He noticed. Isn't it time for us to quit fighting God and instead surrender to Him and His plans?

What keeps you from believing? What keeps you from trusting God?

He promises our weary souls rest, but do you really believe Him? Do you trust that the God of this universe is strong enough to lighten your load? Explain.

In our frailty, many of us don't believe we can be free. If we start to feel defeat and helplessness creeping in, we medicate, we numb out, we order our lives to escape our pain. We seek comfort anywhere we can find it.

Our careers, a prescription, another person's arms.

I can't help but think that our God is looking down at our crippled selves, wanting desperately to rescue us as we wander the streets broken-hearted. Waiting for us to cry out to Him. God is full of compassion and healing, but He won't force Himself on us.

What do you use to numb out or escape pain?

How might your numbing be keeping you from crying out for God's help?

Does your numbness enable you to exist longer in crisis mode than should be humanly possible?

We are born with a large capacity for coping, especially when aided by human mechanisms. Each incident we encounter thickens our skins a little more to take the next blow. The more we medicate, the thicker the skin becomes. Before we know it, we are staring through pain and tragedy with eyes that don't blink, tears that don't come, skin so tough we feel nothing.

I wonder how many women—and men, for that matter—have anesthetized themselves to the world around them in an effort to stop feeling pain. And I wonder how much better off we'd be if we instead embraced our hurts, grief, troubles, and discomfort. If we did, we may not look as put together from the outside. But perhaps we would experience one of life's great paradoxes: we must experience pain in order to experience healing.

I have a friend who recently started taking a common antidepressant. "Vitamin L," she calls it. When she first started taking it, she became concerned that she wasn't able to cry. She tapped her heart, saying, "Is this thing on?" We both laughed. Nervous laughter. I shared her concern. Since then she has found tears again—a relief to her.

For so many people, prescription medication has been a lifesaver in moments of severe struggle, and some people need it to even out imbalances in the brain. However, it's important to consider the implications of a lifetime of medication. For decades I watched my dad take so many medications it made my head spin. Each one prescribed to counteract another. When I saw him a couple of months ago, he was on nine different psychiatric meds.

When I walked into his room, I embraced him and asked, "Hey, Dad, how are you?"

His feeble response: "Numb."

Whether or not we take medication, we all find ways to numb out when we are pressured and stressed.

Perhaps you've been in numbing mode so long you don't allow yourself to *feel* anymore. It hurts too much to look back into your past, to dredge up lonely memories and relive your life's saddest days.

But counter-intuitively, this is where healing begins.

Start by confessing your addictions, your deepest secrets, to someone you trust. When we keep things hidden, we seem put together on the outside, but is that really who we are? When we lay bare our loneliness and isolation, and acknowledge our coping mechanisms, they begin to release their grip on us. Over time, the more we name our struggles, the more they are rendered powerless. We find relief. We begin to feel again.

Come, let us return to the Lord; for he has torn us, that he may heal us; he has struck us down, and he will bind us up.

HOSEA 6:1

When have you experienced healing after a painful time?

What problems can you associate with choosing to "numb out" when you're hurting?

What are the main reasons you would rather hide your hurts than share them?

Hidden

It's easier to run and perform and leave our past exactly there—in our past. We fear that if we reveal all of ourselves, we will be rejected—or worse, discarded. We fear the past will be too painful to dredge up.

But the alternative—a life of hiding, of running—is far worse.

If we keep running from our true selves, we'll continue on a slow and steady spiral to the point where we'll look in the mirror one day and not know our truth from our lies. We won't remember who we truly are.

Secrets have the power to paralyze us as long as they remain locked up deep inside.

In New York, I grew more aware of these hidden losses and started exposing them to the light. I grew comfortable talking about them. Naming my life's defeats became a regular confessional before those who possessed the grace to accept me. And with each sentence of surrender, I found encouragement from these friends to keep digging for more. We encouraged one another to press on, to embrace those hidden layers.

For years my eyes had been closed.

But I was beginning to wake up.

I was discovering the value of living with my eyes wide open.

If we fail to live this way, we will never see the full potential of our futures. For we are shaped by our pasts—our passions, struggles, joys, sorrows, pain—but we need not be defined by it.

Facing our experiences actually sets us free.

We must be willing to encounter the past honestly with a community of trusted friends who will walk with us through the process.

As long as my stories remained hidden, I was in bondage. The more I discovered about my story and myself, the closer I grew toward grasping a sense of meaning.

Sometimes a visual guide helps us see where we've been, what has helped and hurt us along the way, and where we're headed. A life map is a visual path that you create that will guide you to document your life story for the purpose of spiritual growth and a clearer picture of what a life of meaning looks like.

Use this space to draw, write, create, and dig deep
to include those life events that were exhilarating
or devastating. Include names, dates, and details.
What events and pieces of your life story have led
you to where you are and who you are today? Which
people were the most influential in your failures or
successes? What secrets need to be set free? From
what has God delivered you from in the past?

As you look over your map, how have you seen God work and move in your life?

At what point was He working but you couldn't see it at the time?

What painful experiences turned into something beautiful?

What beautiful experiences gave you the most hope and joy?

What qualities do you feel you now possess because of your life experiences?

I think of more stories—so many women walking from a place of bravery. I think of marriages imploding after years of infidelity and watching as grace rushes in. Of families suffering financial ruin and finding provision to rebuild. I'm in awe that I get to befriend these battle-wounded women of beauty. While time and space separates these stories, they are sewn together by a common thread. As I consider these women's lives, a consistent theme surfaces:

Survivors make the most beautiful people.

Our bruises and wounds don't have to make us ugly. They make us who we are. They add texture and color to our lives. They strengthen bonds that might otherwise break. Like others I knew, I'd been plunged into a heart-wrenching difficulty. My life was flush with uncertainty. And yet my heart kept beating. My legs were growing stronger. I was learning much about myself and others and God. I was discovering meaning.

It was terrible and beautiful.

How are you going to use your story—your blessings and bruises—to help someone else? Be specific.

Journal

CHAPTER 5

...

One Life Well Lived

It's God whispering: I am here.
I am true. I am strength.
I love you as you are.
Broken and fragmented.
Let me carry you. Let me
show you a life you never
dreamed or imagined.

For we are God's masterpiece. He has created us anew in Christ Jesus, so we can do the good things he planned for us long ago.
EPHESIANS 2:10, NLT

Don't ask what the world needs. Ask what makes you come alive and go do it, because what the world needs is people who have come alive.
HOWARD THURMAN[1]

Buried

...

adapted excerpts from Chapters 1, 5, 6, and 8 of Freefall to Fly

Take a moment to watch the video, "Finding the Way," by author Rebekah Lyons, available for free at *www.lifeway.com/freefall.*

Too often we live with our talents hidden in the desk drawer. Just out of reach. We've tucked them away. Refusing to listen. So we go on with our lives, not allowing ourselves to go near that drawer.

Not long ago I was burdened to share the truth about embracing our gifts with my eight-year-old son, Pierce. I recounted Jesus' parable of the talents.

Take a moment to read Matthew 25:14-30. Describe a time when you used a gift or talent that God had given you.

Pierce's attention was gripped for a much longer span than usual. I asked him what he thought his talents were. He came up with five, of course, out of his desire to be like the most admired servant. Singing, drawing, building LEGO® towers, playing the guitar, and climbing (preferably rock walls or trees in Central Park).

We decided to draw illustrations of each of these talents and put them on his bulletin board in his bedroom as a reminder that we would commit this eighth year of his life to "investing" in each. Through lessons or focus or skinning up knees, this year would be one for developing those gifts.

A few days after hanging up these illustrations, we spent the holidays with Meeme and Papa (Gabe's parents). With the children gathered around, the grandparents shared stories from decades long past.

Papa shared about his childhood love for art and how he'd earned a scholarship to a specialized art school as a teenager but turned it down. This was news to all of us. Knowing Gabe's love for sketching and Pierce's affinity for drawing ever since he was three, I started connecting the dots as to where these gifts had originated.

Pierce asked Papa why he hadn't attended art school, and Papa responded vaguely: it just wasn't something he would have considered at the time. Times were different then. Families needed feeding, wars needed fighting, and ends needed meeting. Difficult decisions often had to be made based on pragmatism. Papa was raised in a log cabin in the hills of Nelson County, Virginia. He served in the Army during the Vietnam War, found God, and worked for forty years as a welder to provide for a wife and two amazing sons. He rose at 4:00 a.m. for the morning shift every two weeks and worked the night shift until midnight on the others, sacrificing much to provide both his sons a college education.

Pierce, with eight-year-old innocence, asked, "So you buried it, huh?"

Papa looked up, surprised by the pointed honesty of his grandson's question. With a softness in his eyes, he graciously responded, "Well, I guess I did."

What are your "buried" interests?

When Laura's old, heavy door to her eighth-floor apartment swung open, I felt welcomed into a safe haven. Though the whole place was bathed in cozy warmth, I always angled for a seat on her worn, chocolate leather couch. The knocking sound emanating from her prewar radiators was a metronome that placed me at ease. Even on the chilliest days, it meant the heat was here to stay.

We'd spent our fall conversations in tears and confessions, awakening to our hidden struggles with these trusted few gathered in Laura's apartment, but this new year we were moving forward. We gathered weekly around books and discussion, learning through each other's experiences and promptings.

One morning as I read at home in preparation for our next meeting, I was riveted by a quote in Ann Voskamp's book *One Thousand Gifts*:

> Hands of the clock whip hard. So I push hard and I bark hard and I fall hard and when their wide eyes brim sadness and their chins tremble weak, I am weary and I am the thin clear skin, reflecting their fatigue. . . . The hurry makes us hurt.[2]

I collapsed on the floor in heartbreak. I recalled Pierce's quivering lip just three days prior as I yelled at him to get out the door. To church. Where his father was teaching that day. My hypocrisy slapped me in the face. I kept reading:

> "Wherever you are, be all there." I have lived the runner, panting ahead in worry, pounding back in regrets, terrified to live in the present, because here-time asks me to do the hardest of all: just open wide and receive. . . . I just want time to do my one life well.[3]

This reminder of reality caused me to pause. *What am I so afraid of? Why is living in the moment so difficult?*

How would you answer those questions?

For me, when the busy stops and the hurry fades, I'm left with a haunting feeling of inadequacy. All my efforts, no matter how much I try, are never enough. So I keep returning to that hamster wheel, chasing after a feeling of worth. But the opposite was happening instead. The running was prohibiting my heart from opening wide to receive meaning. The hurry was making me hurt.

We're not called to stay on a hamster wheel. We're called to stop and to seek refuge from God. In fact, we live best when we stay close to God.

Come to me, all who labor and are heavy laden, and I will give you rest. Take my yoke upon you, and learn from me, for I am gentle and lowly in heart, and you will find rest for your souls. For my yoke is easy, and my burden is light.

MATTHEW 11:28-30

The Lord is my shepherd; I shall not want.
He makes me lie down in green pastures.
He leads me beside still waters.
He restores my soul.
He leads me in paths of righteousness
for his name's sake.

PSALM 23:1-3

What things make you feel burdened? Inadequate?

What keeps you from being present for those who
need you? From seeing the blessings in front of you?

Who in your life has suffered when you have been
unable to live in the moment?

I had been living a life of scarcity, a life of not-enoughs, until I learned how
to accept and focus on the blessings of God. Funny how I had overlooked
the generosity of life until I started looking for it—by naming the gifts in
my midst. So I wrote down my gifts and simple delights. As I penned my
gratitude list, my heart changed. The more blessings I listed, the more
I noticed. I was discovering how to live this one life well.

What simple delights have you been taking for granted?
Create your gratitude list below.

Treasure

...

I never recognized my passion for stories until thirty-five years into living. No one pointed it out. We are often oblivious until others point to such things and name them. With my girlfriends' words fresh in my mind—"Your love for stories is part of your giftedness"—I lugged a stack of paperback friends with me.

During our first day by the pool, I cracked open *The Alchemist* by Paulo Coelho, a fable set in premodern times about a boy named Santiago who goes on a grueling search for treasure and meaning.

I couldn't put it down.

Santiago encounters many hardships and finds a little love on his expedition, but he never loses focus of what he seeks. His confidence is rooted in the belief that treasure awaits him. If only he can stay alive long enough to discover it. So he sets about on a journey. Against all odds. Willing to sacrifice whatever is necessary in order to find it.

I saw myself in young Santiago. He believed his rousing voyage would lead him to a lifelong treasure. Without realizing it, I had been on a rigorous search for my own elusive treasure most of my adult life. I'd longed for meaning that transcended circumstance. But unlike Santiago, my journey had been confounded by doubt. Was I willing to undergo anything to find what I was looking for? The hope of something more and the ideal of what might lie ahead flittered in the distance like an oasis in the desert.

As the breeze blew in over the cliffs, I hugged my towel closer. Reclining in my chair, I closed my eyes and pondered a simple question: *What treasure am I seeking?*

Is it a bigger house, trophy kids, a new car, a fulfilling career, a lifestyle of material possessions? Would these things finally bring me happiness? Would they give me meaning?

What treasures are you seeking?

What fulfillment have those things brought you?
Is it lasting?

As in *The Alchemist*, the topic of treasure seeking makes a prominent appearance in the Bible, as well. I remembered a story from the Gospel of Matthew where Jesus teaches His disciples a few cornerstone principles about treasure. He explains that storing up earthly treasures is a worthless endeavor. Houses, money, livestock—they all rust or are eaten by moths. Destroyed by the same decay that haunts this world. But then Jesus describes a different kind of treasure. He implores His followers,

> Don't store up treasures here on earth, where moths eat them and rust destroys them, and where thieves break in and steal. Store your treasures in heaven, where moths and rust cannot destroy, and thieves do not break in and steal. Wherever your treasure is, there the desires of your heart will also be.

MATTHEW 6:19-21, NLT

We can spend our lives focusing on things that will never bring us fulfillment. Or we can trust in God and cling to that which is precious.

> The kingdom of heaven is like a merchant in search of fine pearls, who, on finding one pearl of great value, went and sold all that he had and bought it.

MATTHEW 13:45-46

A fortune that will last.
Where no thief can ever steal or rust destroy.
Sealed in perpetuity.
This was a treasure worth scouting for. I lay there spellbound.
Awakened to the truth that my real treasure would look vastly different

from what the world had led me to believe. I knew firsthand that material treasures could never quench my thirsty soul. They always left me wanting. And yet I couldn't help myself. We are by nature a people who like to store stuff. We make games of it. Advertise it. Get high achieving it. Shiny, sparkly possessions are everywhere we turn, and we feel ourselves being drawn to them. Even as we find more items to fill our treasure chests, we sense the moths eating, the rust corroding, and the gleam fading faster than we can preserve them. So off we go in search for more.

I have felt the fading in my own life. Striving to accomplish more by having more. Living a life of *never enough*. Trying to fill the void left by my struggle for purpose with things that fade away. Battling a lifelong struggle with anxiety and despair. My earthly treasures leaving me pining for more.

In what ways have you given into the belief of never having enough?

After meeting Santiago, I began to think about Jesus' teaching in a new light. What would it look like to find treasure that is eternal rather than temporal, intangible rather than material, lasting rather than fleeting? Then it hit me like a flash of light:

What if eternal treasure is engaging what God uniquely created you to do? By stewarding the gifts you've been uncovering? By becoming the person you were designed to be?

For where your treasure is, there your heart will be also.

MATTHEW 6:21

If we invest in earthly treasures, Jesus seemed to be saying, our hearts will shrivel with them. When we derive meaning from fleeting objects, our spirits decay and become a meal for moths. But if we invest in eternal treasures, our hearts will be satisfied. My recent struggles confirmed the truth in His words.

As I began to journal my thoughts, two sentences leaped off my pen:
Earthly treasure shrivels.
Eternal treasure satisfies.

Name three things you can do to focus on the satisfaction of eternal treasures instead of earthly treasures?

1.

2.

3.

Most of my adult life, I'd been searching for the wrong treasure. As a result, I'd lost touch with who I was designed to be. I'd abandoned my natural bent somewhere along the way due to the pressure of responsibility and the pressure from others. I traded in my desire to use the gifts God gave me and instead became the person everyone else expected me to be. I had grasped for what the world told me was valuable. And somewhere along the way, I'd stopped believing that true treasure—God's intended responsibility for me—even existed in the first place.

How have you traded your gifts and worked instead to develop into someone others expect you to be?

Mulling over this concept of treasure, I wondered, *Which is more despairing? That our treasure from God exists and we can't find it? Or that it never really existed in the first place?* Think on that.

I had to believe the former was worse. Perhaps we are less grieved if we go through life without giving much thought to the thing we are missing. But the pain bred from searching and longing for a treasure that seems to always elude us is devastating.

On the other hand, once we realize that this treasure exists, we can begin the process of finding it. I'd always sensed my treasure might be locked away in a chest on the other side of the world, but perhaps it sat right in front of my face, just needing recognition. It existed because I existed. My Creator stored it up for me. Uniquely Rebekah. Before I was born, along with a crowning inheritance. My treasure was there all along, even before I knew to search for it.

What lengths are you willing to go to in order to find the satisfying eternal treasure found in Scripture?

Take some time to read through these two parables. Jot down your thoughts on each as you read them.

☐ **Matthew 25:14-29**

☐ **Luke 12:13-21**

If we're honest, being given even more responsibility when we're faithful with what we have—and are often overwhelmed with—doesn't exactly sound appealing. Yet focusing on others and what we can do for them—instead of ourselves—is exactly where we discover the longings of our heart—peace, joy, and contentment. Giving of ourselves feels good (see Acts 20:35). It helps us find meaning in the mundane. It reveals godly treasures that we often can't find within ourselves. Yet we have to be careful that we use our blessings where God has called us to serve.

Direction

...

In our zeal to lay hold of what others seem to have, we go through seasons of searching. But after a while, we grow weary. It's exhausting, this treasure hunting. So we slide into a most depressing spiral. After some time we stop looking because the cost is too great. Too painful. And we're not quite sure it's worth it. Or that it even exists.

My time in New York had zapped my spirit, but my heart was being revived. I sensed that treasure did exist. It looked different than I'd once thought but treasure was indeed waiting for me. Promising to fill my empty heart, just like Jesus said.

What if God wants to lead us toward the discovery of that treasure?

What if, instead of searching alone, we were meant to have Him walk along-side us and show us the way? Reminding us that He created us with these gifts?

His eyes have watched everything, from our earliest days, and have borne witness to the battle wounds that now mark our bodies. And yet He tenderly loves us and carries us and whispers to us that the treasure is not as far away as we might think. That the journey to find it is long and hard because of our weariness, not because it's beyond reach. Not because it doesn't exist.

If only we would let Him lead. What journey would He take us on to discover it?

So we keep walking, because He is the One who planted that treasure in the first place. He created it. He is bringing us back to it. He is increasing our faith, step by step, and we are climbing and believing. And the closer we get, the more certain we become. Why is this search different from any other we have undergone? Why so much simpler? Perhaps because we aren't pulling. We are being pulled. We are being led to discover our purpose—our bliss.

What is your bliss?

I wondered, *What in the world is my bliss?* I thought of all the pleasures I'd loved and enjoyed over the years. Experiences I would gladly do for free. Decorating and redecorating, hosting parties, fashion styling, shopping, making music, or just listening to it, for that matter—a bliss of beauty and order. All great gifts. But for some reason when I'd entered this season in New York, none of these pleasures were satisfying anymore. I found myself falling, and no amount of parties, aesthetics, or symphonic rhythms could stop me. This led me to an even scarier question: *What is my greatest fear?*

What is your fear?

Conjuring the courage to remember, I thought back to my toughest moments of the past year. As I walked the forlorn Manhattan streets that first autumn and winter, I realized my greatest fear was waking up every morning to a life of mental illness. A life of struggle, anxiety, and depression. I never planned for this. I worked hard to create a perception of having life together with my fancy decorating and party throwing, but the low hum I'd sensed in Georgia was now roaring loudly in my ears. Up moments and dreaded down moments. I realized that for years my bliss covered my greatest fear. Until the pressure cooker of this new reality forced it to the surface.

My bliss had been a distraction from my fear.

I hadn't once considered how my story might relate to others who struggle through the same internal battles. Many women look so buttoned up on the outside, but this journey taught me that all of us have a lot more going on under the surface than we let others see. If my story was any indication of what one in four women my age was feeling, then I must do my part to help.

Maybe, just maybe, my story mattered.

As Gabe and I conversed over salad and flatbread pizzas, every experience I'd undergone in the past couple of years came into focus. My heart broke from knowing so many women who faced these same fears and anxieties.

What if my gifts are meant to illuminate my own story of struggle? What if my burden is meant to help others walk through their own difficult journeys? What if my surrender is the gateway to finding meaning in my life?

I was left with no choice but to talk about this struggle openly, honestly, embarrassingly. Women shouldn't have to feel they are alone. We need each other's stories; we need to know we can survive and become beautiful people.

I had a responsibility to share this with others.

What responsibilities do you have to other Christians? To other unbelievers?

What is your story? And how do you sense God leading you to share it with others?

In Galatians 6, Paul reminds believers that we are to restore those caught in any wrongdoing with a gentle spirit. Our minds automatically go to the worst of "wrongdoing." But what if the wrongdoing is disobedience to God? Ignoring His calling and gifting on your life?

Bear one another's burdens.

GALATIANS 6:2

How has another person's story helped you through a difficult time?

What lengths would you go to in order to share your story of finding treasure and to help others discover their treasures and gifts?

Purpose

This year of discovering my gifts and sharing my struggle birthed new meaning in me as a few lasting truths became clear:

Meaning awakens when we realize our gifts. Meaning is fulfilled when our story finds purpose. Calling is where your talents and your burdens collide. Once we know what we're good at, our gifts, we must match those things with a deep need in this world, our burdens.

What's a memory that makes you weep on quiet nights? What heartache creeps up on you when no one else is around?

When you discover this, you will know your deepest burden.

Out of all the brokenness in this world, how can we single out just one? I learned that my burden is directly related to my story. Your burden may be much the same and directly relate to your story. Look back at your map—the road you've walked as long as you can remember. Think about the turning points and changes that marked patterns of joy and patterns of pain.

As you go through your life, dig in. You will start to see where your burden is unveiled by the moments that have caused you pain. Because you walked through those dark moments, empathy compels you toward others walking a similar road.

My patterns of pain came in the form of a mental struggle with anxiety and depression. A long history I'm now embracing. While I still struggle, those emotions no longer wield the same power over me. Instead, I use them to break my heart for those who tread the same path. My passion has become helping women find their callings, helping them live their stories fully and deeply.

Each of us must find our own path to totter down as we seek to live out our purpose. We must find those God-gifts that make us uniquely us, and then pair them with a burden that those gifts fit like a key. When we do, rescue will flood into our lives. And in the deluge, we'll begin to discover meaning.

What would you say are your gifts? Or even better, what gifts do others see in you?

What is your burden? What are most passionate about? What gives you a sense of responsibility or duty?

How have you used your gifts to help someone else? How can you do this again in the future?

Describe a time you have used your burden, your passion, your heartache to help someone else. How can you do this again in the future?

Read from Ephesians 2 and think about its meaning. Reflect on your purpose and what it means to live your life well, pondering what God may have planned for you.

> For we are his workmanship, created in Christ
> Jesus for good works, which God prepared
> beforehand, that we should walk in them.
>
> EPHESIANS 2:10

God has planned for believers to do good works as a result and as evidence of their salvation. Good works follow salvation. Other Scriptures clearly say that there is no way your good works make you worthy of salvation (see Gal. 2:21; Phil. 3:9; 2 Tim. 1:9; Titus 3:5). You are not saved by good works but for good works. Remember our calling is where our gifts and our burdens collide.

> **What are the good works God has called you to accomplish?**

> **What might God have in store for you as you walk with Him and fulfill His plans and purpose?**

The prophet Jeremiah says,

> For I know the plans I have for you, declares the LORD, plans for welfare and not for evil, to give you a future and a hope. Then you will call upon me and come and pray to me, and I will hear you. You will seek me and find me, when you seek me with all your heart.
>
> **JEREMIAH 29:11-13**

These verses from a letter written by Jeremiah for God's people as they were exiled reminded them that God had a plan. God was the One who would restore His people. This hopeful message went to God's people while they were in the midst of what appeared to be a hopeless situation. God promised eventual restoration. He promised them a hope and a future. Like these exiles who hung onto hope knowing that God was Sovereign, we too, can cling to His promises and know that He has a purpose for the gifts, the talents, the burdens, and the calling He has placed on our lives.

Tweet what you're learning: *#freefalltofly*

CHAPTER 6

...

Calling & Called

Let me take you on a journey so
marvelous you point back to Me.
Let me rename you.
Let me bring you back to your
truest self. The way I ordered
you from the beginning.
All this, for My glory.

The thief's purpose is to steal and kill and destroy.
My purpose is to give them a rich and satisfying life.
JOHN 10:10, NLT

We often think calling comes from following our bliss,
but it actually comes from following our greatest fear.
BOBETTE BUSTER[1]

Remember

adapted excerpts from Chapter 9 and the Postlude of Freefall to Fly

Take a moment to watch the video, "Birthright Gifts," by author Rebekah Lyons, available for free at *www.lifeway.com/freefall.*

It's one thing to read another person's story and sense possibility, but it's another to decide you are ready to take the leap. Although we travel different paths, most of us end up in a place of longing at one point or another. Some women have pursued their dreams yet experienced incredible pain when life didn't work out the way they planned. For others, life worked out exactly how they planned, but when they got what they wanted, they realized they were not fulfilled.

Pain and emptiness.

From lives planned and chaotic.

Facing our pain or emptiness head-on is no easy task. I often ask myself, *Who am I to shine light?* I'm still grieving this mess like everyone else. My vagabond mess. I have been crushed with these questions: With all this suffering in people's lives, how do we get back up? How does our struggle turn to light?

In the eyes of other women like me, I've noticed the desire to push through. But the *how* overwhelms us.

How do we find meaning?

I now know that we must start by remembering. Before the children came, before the marriage began, before high school graduation, before the loss of whatever happened . . . when did your heart sing? Did you lie on your back, barefoot in the meadow at dusk, looking up at the vastness of the stars? Did you find yourself enraptured that a Creator ordered these stars one by one and knows each of them by name? Did you imagine how great you are to God's heart while feeling so small within this cosmos? Did your spirit soar with a glimpse of heartfelt delight from Him?

Can you even remember it? That fullness so great you felt as if you'd burst? That moment when you felt the presence of God in your midst. How long has it been since you felt that again? How long has it been since that fullness broke through your ordinary day and brought you to your knees? How long have you been shackled in bondage, where the wounds are too great?

The new normal is a life of survival. And survival means that dreams die. Whoever said that life is not big enough for *all* God's fullness? What lies have we believed that said we are not worthy? That He is not capable?

Are there dreams you buried as life went on and disappointment hit? What were they?

Write down your earliest dreams.

For most of us, God has been weaving a story full of ebbs and flows. The successes and failures, the significant others, mentors, and friends along with the disappointing, confidence-shattering relationships. They all have purpose. Each experience preparing us for the next.

You've been walking down a path, and at times your entire life has turned on a dime when you experienced a particular moment. A lesson learned. A dream pursued. These moments lead you to a destination, if you will muster the courage to stare down the road, into the horizon. What have been the major turning points in your life?

What are some of the major turning points in your life?

We all have talents. Sometimes hidden and other times on display for everyone to see. Often we don't feel confident enough to affirm them ourselves. We need others to name them for us. These birthright gifts were given to us by God. They are what make us uniquely ourselves.

Recalling from the last chapter, what is your greatest bliss and how have you used it to help someone?

I learned that my burden is directly related to my story. The road I've walked as long as I remember. The turning points continually changing my trajectory. Changes that marked patterns of joy and patterns of pain.

As you go through your own life, dig in. You will start to see where your burden is unveiled by the moments that have caused you pain. Because you walked through those dark moments, empathy compels you toward others walking a similar road.

> So then, since we have a great High Priest who has entered heaven, Jesus the Son of God, let us hold firmly to what we believe. This High Priest of ours understands our weaknesses, for he faced all of the same testings we do, yet he did not sin. So let us come boldly to the throne of our gracious God. There we will receive his mercy, and we will find grace to help us when we need it most.
>
> **HEBREWS 4:14-16, NLT**

Because Jesus was fully human, He empathizes with us in every way. On earth, Jesus faced a multitude of temptations, trials, and suffering. He endured sorrow, stress, and being overwhelmed. Yet He remained sinless. It's also during those difficult times when He turned to God for help.

We are wise to do the same.

In our weakness, God is strong. Through our burdens, His glory is revealed.

Search for the greatest burdens buried in your heart. What keeps you up at night and shakes you awake in the morning? What makes you cry, and what makes you dance?

Look for the moments when you feel most afraid or when the injustices you see around you stir up anger.

For me, my greatest fear was mental illness, and my burden was for women who are fading.

Again looking over your journal, what is your greatest burden and how have you used it to help someone?

No matter our age or life stage, as women we share many common principles. I uncovered some of these during a retreat with Pete Richardson, a
life-planning coach and Gabe's longtime mentor. Over two days at the Ace
Hotel's boardroom off Broadway and 29th, he helped me and several other
women gain clarity on our callings.

Finally, the purpose of this journey was coming together.

So there I sat with Pete, intimidated yet eager before the first word—
ready to chart my path. Pete has led more than six hundred people
through this process, so his expertise wasn't lost on me. With an oversize
moleskin journal and a pencil in hand, I was a captive audience.

He began, "We each have an assignment from God. The question is
whether we know it."

Even if I wasn't sure I had a calling, Pete was convinced. I decided to
move past the *if* of calling and focus on the *what*. Overcoming my fear
of mental neurosis catapulted me to this place, but knowing what I was
meant to do would complete it.

After having us chart the major turning points in our lives and looking
for the consistent themes, Pete had us settle in on the arc of our stories.
I gained clarity about my God-given talents and even unveiled my deepest
burdens from the past two years. My gifts were becoming clearer—writing,
offering counsel, being resourceful, creating inviting environments—and
so were my burdens, as my heart broke for women who lived shackled and
in need of freedom.

I was reminded that one of my heroes, Viktor Frankl, believed anxiety
was "due to [a person's] sense of unfulfilled responsibility and a lack of
meaning."[2] If I was to sustain or even complete this journey, fulfilling my
responsibility would be critical.

Meaning

Through grueling excavating sessions, I dug deep to provide a descriptive statement of just what my responsibility might be. Every word counted. Letting out a deep breath, I wrote down the following words:

> My calling is to empower women to name and identify
> their struggles and walk with them as they find healing
> and transformation.

My heartbeat quickened to a rapid pace. Warmth flooded my soul. There it sat on paper—the mission of my life. How far had I traveled to discover the treasure that was buried deep inside me? How long had I endured nights of panicked cries for rescue? All those experiences had led to this moment. These words encapsulated the "why" of this entire journey.

The moment of final surrender had found rescue. And that rescue unveiled my highest calling, grounding my life in my deepest meaning. My struggle found purpose.

Spend time in silence working on a statement that combines your bliss with your burden. Don't worry about grammar or brilliance. Just get it on paper.

Now write out a plan for how you are going to use this to help someone else.

Life exists in seasons. Solomon once wrote,

For everything there is a season, and a time for every matter under heaven.

ECCLESIASTES 3:1

Seasons to change diapers, breast-feed, toilet train, spoon-feed. But what if meaning is more than that? Of course I'm called to be a mother—just as Gabe is called to be a father. But if I'm not careful, I lose my identity. I become defined by something outside myself. I cease to be Rebekah, the uniquely talented woman made in God's image. I'm now only Rebekah, wife of Gabe. Or Rebekah, mother of Cade, Pierce, and Kennedy. I love these roles, but I also recognize that deriving one's identity from another person is a short road to resentment.

God intended for me to contribute my birthright gifts to the world.

I wonder if women like me hide behind our husbands, our unfulfilling jobs, or even motherhood because we're afraid of embracing the full person God has created us to be.

What if the transformation hurts?

What if I find I'm not good at anything else?

What if I fail?

Could our desires to satisfy the expectations of others and play it safe be keeping us from the full meaning God has for us?

What things have you been hiding behind?

I'm not suggesting that we give up on our families and go make our dreams come true. Quite the opposite. Women must discover their callings precisely because the health of their families, relationships, and communities is so vital. When we become who we're meant to be, everyone around us benefits. When we live out the stories God wants to tell through us, we bring healing to all who struggle alongside us.

How are we able to do this?

Read through the following verses. As you read
each passage, write how it can be used as an
encouragement to live out your purpose in the world.

Psalm 63:1-4

Acts 1:8

Romans 12:1-5

2 Corinthians 1:3-6

Ephesians 3:14-20

Ephesians 5:1

Philippians 2:12-16

Let's read part of that 2 Corinthians passage one more time:

> Blessed be the God and Father of our Lord Jesus Christ, the Father of mercies and God of all comfort, who comforts us in all our affliction, so that we may be able to comfort those who are in any affliction, with the comfort with which we ourselves are comforted by God.
>
> 2 CORINTHIANS 1:3-4

The apostle Paul, the author of 2 Corinthians, found that intense pressures from life led him to depend further on God for direction, patience, endurance, and comfort.

What is your most common response to pressure? Does it deepen your walk with God or distance you?

What role can you play in helping others face their burdens? In allowing them to do the same for you?

Connection
...

God gives us our purpose and then He equips us to carry it out. It's up to us to listen and learn from Him through prayer and time spent in His Word. It's up to us to embrace fully the power of the Holy Spirit that He gives us as a gift when we surrender our lives to Him through salvation. It's all there. We just have to seek, find, and carry out what is waiting for us.

Yet sometimes it takes others to help us identify our calling. To live out our purpose. Because we were never meant to do anything alone.

> When two of you get together on anything at all on earth and make a prayer of it, my Father in heaven goes into action. And when two or three of you are together because of me, you can be sure that I'll be there.
>
> MATTHEW 18:19-20, MSG

In what ways have your life experiences prepared you to help someone else?

In what areas do you have the most to offer in terms of Christian growth?

God has imagined specific intentions for each and every woman in the world. Our Creator has a vast imagination, and with that divine intelligence He's given us all birthright gifts. We don't have to look to the right or the left on this. We don't have to copy or compete or compare because there's enough fullness in the kingdom that we can all be deployed on what we're wired for, to lean into what our natural bent is.

The families we've been born into. The stories we've walked. The journeys we've led. There's such beauty in that variety. All we need to do is play our individual parts. To uplift those in our circle of impact. To remind others that we are for them. To affirm them. If we all really owned and embodied the fullness of what walking in our callings meant and celebrated our gifts from God, then there's no limit to what God would do. Working together with the people you love will give God exponential reach.

As iron sharpens iron, so a friend sharpens a friend.

PROVERBS 27:17, NLT

When we explore questions about our purpose in the context of a friendship between those who really know and love each other well, we become the iron that sharpens iron.

What kind of spiritual maturity do you think happens best in community, rather than in solitude?

In what ways do you think your life will be benefited by pursuing a mentoring relationship?

Help identify passions and hobbies in those around you. Ask the hard questions: *What is your story? Why is this such a passion for you? How is it connected to this? Why is this something you can't seem to shake?* Then work together to know *why* you need to use those giftings. Because the why is actually informed by *what* breaks your heart. Where you've experienced wounding. Where you've suffered. Where you've grieved. Where you've been rejected or abandoned. And when you know that, that's where the healing comes. When God walks you into freedom.

Joy
...

As I embrace this life of meaning, living fully with the remaining days I am given, my laundry and dishes pile high. My inbox sits unattended. Dinner ranges from toaster waffles to pot roast. But no matter the cleanliness or the menu, my greatest joys are laughter and conversation, whether it's simply our family of five or our larger community of friends delighting in each other. We come as we are. Fully vulnerable and accepted. At family bedtime, we exchange confessions for forgiveness. Talents are affirmed, and dreams are encouraged.

I'm living from a new place. Not from a place of perception, but of vulnerability. A place of rescue. A place of surrender. It's overwhelming and scary, and I can't imagine life any other way.

Look around you. And then look inside you. Maybe you're asking the same question I've wondered for a long time.

Can we really have it all?

How do you respond to the question, *Can we really have it all?*

As I consider my journey, I cautiously respond yes. But not in the way one might think. It's not having a perfect house or a larger salary or smarter children or acquiring more stuff. It's not completing a task list. It's not looking perfect. Or being perfect.

It's a plan derailed,

a life surrendered,

a bondage broken.

It's knowing *who* you are. And more important, knowing *Whose* you are. It's using your gifts for the rescue of others and not living in fear. And then affirming these truths to the loved ones in your midst.

So let's change the question.

Do you really want it all? Do you want the joy, the pain, the plan—or the plan derailed? Will you welcome the life that takes you off course? Explain.

Because if you do, you will truly live. You will be fully alive. Awakened to a life of reckless abandon, where you bare your heart and soul and you don't look back. Where you run wild and free from the bondage of fear. Where you laugh and delight in the place of freedom. Where you live with courage because you have been rescued.

Over these last two years, I've learned that you can't take flight without a freefall. So if you're standing on the edge of your own cliff wondering what to do, just leap.

I promise. It's worth it.

I recall saying a year ago that I would live a life of brokenness no matter the cost, so long as it kept me dependent on God. So much of me wanted to be shiny and funny, but this new place keeps me aware of my failures and struggles. Not to be swept up by them, but to let Him rescue, again and again. So I'm thankful for the continual crying out. Anything else feels counterfeit. I know it appears odd, but I'm okay with it.

Perhaps this oddness extends beyond what we ask for and closer to what we long for.

To be undone and swept up in His presence.

To surrender our heads and our hearts.

To tell stories of rescue and redemption.

To be held captive to the life we only think we control.

To be freed to live the life He ordered for us in the first place.

God, You are drawing near. We can tell. May we fall in Your arms on this journey toward a life of meaning.

Tweet what you're learning: #freefalltofly

Journal

· · ·

Endnotes

Chapter 1
1. Saint Augustine, *Confessions,* Book 1, Par. 1

Chapter 2
1. Yvonne Pierre, *The Day My Soul Cried* (Marietta, GA: Zyonair's Unlimited, 2010).

Chapter 3
1. Oswald Chambers, "December 31," *My Utmost for His Highest* (Uhrichsville, OH: Barbour Publishing, Inc., 1963).
2. Marianne Williamson, *A Return to Love: Reflections on the Principles of a Course in Miracles* (New York: HarperCollins, 1992), 190-191.
3. Reginald F. Christian, ed., *Tolstoy's Letters,* vol. 2 (New York: Scribners, 1978), n.p.

Chapter 4
1. C.S. Lewis, *Mere Christianity* (New York: HarperOne, 1980), 147.

Chapter 5
1. Howard Thurman, *Howard Thurman Center for Common Ground,* Boston University. Online. Accessed September 2, 2014. Available at *www.bu.edu/thurman/about/history.*
2. Ann Voskamp, *One Thousand Gifts* (Grand Rapids, MI: Zondervan, 2010), 66-69.
3. Ibid.

Chapter 6
1. Bobbette Buster, "Epiphany: The Art of Transformational Narrative" (lecture, Crosby Street Hotel, New York, October 2011).
2. C. George Boeree, "Viktor Frankl," *Personality Theories.* Online. Accessed September 2, 2014. Available at *http://webspace.ship.edu/cgboer/frankl.html.*

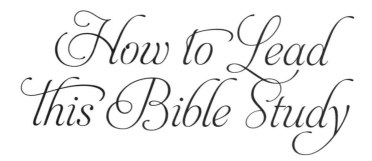

How to Lead this Bible Study

Whether you are just starting a Bible study or continuing to grow groups in your church, we are so grateful for your investment in the lives of women and that you have chosen LifeWay studies, and specifically, *Freefall to Fly* by Rebekah Lyons. These studies can be used in a variety of settings including church settings, homes, office buildings, coffee shops, or other locations you secure. So where do you begin?

PRAY. Pray, pray. As you prepare for leading this Bible study know that prayer is essential. Spend time asking God to work in the hearts and lives of women who will participate in the study. Begin now learning what issues the women are facing and praying about what will help them grow spiritually. Continue to pray throughout the study and encourage the women to include prayer as a daily spiritual discipline. Pray for God to lead you to women He is calling to help you lead your small groups.

TALK TO YOUR PASTOR OR MINISTER OF EDUCATION. Ask for their input, prayers, and support.

SECURE YOUR LOCATION. Think about the number of women you can accommodate in the designated location. Reserve any tables, chairs, or needed media equipment for watching the free videos from Rebekah at *www.lifeway.com/freefall*.

PROVIDE CHILDCARE. If you are targeting moms of young children and/or single moms, this is essential.

PROVIDE RESOURCES. Order the needed number of member books. You might get a few extra for last minute drop-ins.

PLAN AND PREPARE. Become familiar with the Bible study. Preview the videos from Rebekah at *www.lifeway.com/freefall*. Prepare the outline you will follow to lead the group meeting based on the leader helps available. Go to *www.lifeway.com* to find free extra leader resources.

LEAD. One of the best things you can do as the leader is set the pace for this study. Be consistent and trustworthy. Encourage the women to follow through on the study, to attend the group sessions, and hold one another accountable to do their reading between sessions. Accept women where they are but also set expectations that motivate commitment. Listen carefully and be responsible with the discussions and sharing within the group. Keep confidences shared within the group. Be honest and vulnerable with the group and share what God is teaching you. Most women will follow your lead and be more willing to share and participate when they see your example.

FOLLOW UP BETWEEN SESSIONS. Throughout the study stay engaged with the women. Use social media, emails, or even a quick note in the mail to connect with the group and share prayer needs. Let them know when you are praying specifically for them. Root everything in Scripture and encourage them in their relationship with Jesus.

CELEBRATE AND SHARE. As a group, share what God has taught each one and where lives have been transformed. Pray together about what commitment God is asking from them as a result of this study.

EVALUATE. What went well? What could be improved upon? Did you see women's lives transformed? Were your small group leaders effective?

NEXT STEPS. Even after the study concludes follow up and challenge women to stay involved with others through another Bible study, church opportunities, or anything that will continue their spiritual growth and friendships. Provide several options of ministry and/or mission opportunities the members can participate in individually or as a group to apply what they have learned through this study.

Thank you again for serving the Lord by pouring into the lives of women.

Leader Guide

The following suggestions can give you ideas for leading a *Freefall to Fly* Bible study group. The point of a group study is to support each other as you apply God's Word to your lives. Always take the suggestions as a place to start, but pray and complete your own study. Since every group is different, and since you have unique strengths and weaknesses, combine these suggestions with your creativity to find the best way to conduct a group.

Each chapter's material will read like a book with room for the group to write their own responses and thoughts. Encourage them to stop at any point that they read a question, Bible verse, or paragraph that stirs conviction so that they can ponder and pray through the things that God is doing in their hearts.

To hear more of Rebekah's story, read the entire book, *Freefall to Fly: A Breathtaking Journey Toward a Life of Meaning* (Tyndale House Publishers).

Promoting the Group Study

Promote the group through church bulletin announcements, posters, community announcements, social media, and personal invitation. At *www.lifeway.com/freefall* you will find downloadable promotion helps.

A Six-Week Group Plan

The suggested plan is for a six-session group experience. However, you may custom design the group experience to fit the needs of your group and/or church. Distribute books and instruct group members to read through the first chapter before the first session, taking time to process each question. Then the group will work as follows:

Session 1: Discuss the questions and journal entries from Chapter 1. Between group sessions, members will read and process Chapter 2.

Session 2: Discuss the questions and journal entries from Chapter 2. Between group sessions, members will read and process Chapter 3.

Session 3: Discuss the questions and journal entries from Chapter 3. Between group sessions, members will read and process Chapter 4.

Session 4: Discuss the questions and journal entries from Chapter 4. Between group sessions, members will read and process Chapter 5.

Session 5: Discuss the questions and journal entries from Chapter 5. Between group sessions, members will read and process Chapter 6.

Session 6: Discuss the questions and journal entries from Chapter 6. Wrap up the study and determine what's next.

Before Each Group Session

Complete the chapter you will cover in your next group time. Make notes of anything your group may need to further clarify. After the introductory week, complete the questions in the study guide for the next discussion. As you read, select the questions you believe your group will want to discuss. Draw from the questions posed throughout the chapters and the questions provided in this leader guide. Pray about what goals the session most needs to meet for your group, and plan your session to accomplish those goals.

Remain open to the Spirit's leadership. Sometimes a group member will come with a concern or question that will result in a wonderful group experience that will bless the entire group. Other times you may need to avoid letting someone hijack the group into side issues. Experience and reliance on the Spirit will help you to know the difference. You will probably find that you will never get it right every time. If the group members are getting into the material, praying, and studying Scripture, your leadership will bear fruit.

GROUP SESSION 1

Life Unsettled

...

Welcome the group. Ask what insights members have encountered in their study this week. Lead the discussion, drawing from the following suggested questions, or if the women volunteer insights, simply guide the sharing.

Suggested Discussion Questions
- □ What drew you to this study?
- □ What does the phrase "freefall to fly" mean to you?

Take a moment to watch the introductory video, "The Crash & Burn," by author Rebekah Lyons, available for free at *www.lifeway.com/freefall*. Even if participants watched the video during their personal study, it will be beneficial to review as a group.

- □ When have you found yourself in a tug-of-war between two directions in your life? (p. 11) What did you give up? What did you gain?

Ask a volunteer to read Psalm 57:1-3.

- □ What emotions did you sense in David? (p. 13)
- □ Rebekah says, "Sometimes we need a freefall to teach us how to fly." What scares you the most about a freefall? (p. 14)
- □ Read Psalm 42. What specific verses in this psalm resonate with you and why? (p. 17)
- □ Rebekah spoke about her firstborn having Down syndrome. What situations or circumstances have put you on a detour that completely altered what you thought God had planned? (pp. 17-18)
- □ How did the situation change your hope for the future? (p. 18)

☐ What are some specific ways that you desperately try to keep control of your life? (p. 19) What role does failure play in your attempt to control these things?

☐ How might fear be holding you back from accomplishing something you've longed to achieve? (p. 21)

Ask a volunteer to read Psalm 115:11.

☐ How can this verse encourage you to let go of the fear of what God desires to do in your life? (p. 21)

☐ How might your life change if you lean into the Lord more and trust Him for your good? (p. 21)

Ask volunteers to read Genesis 1:27; Isaiah 43:7; and Jeremiah 1:5.

☐ What strikes you most about these verses? (p. 23)

☐ What dreams have you put on hold? (p. 24)

☐ What ideas, things, or habits will you need to let go of in order to begin your freefall?

Prayer & Closing

Spend some time in silence thanking God for the remarkable job He did creating you for a purpose. Ask Him to reveal to you the qualities about yourself that you need to treasure and claim as His gifts to you. Ask Him to show you how to draw closer to Him and commit to a deeper relationship with Him. Pray for others in your group, asking the Lord to guide this group as you continue this incredible journey of discovery together.

Finding yourself and truly living is a process that can't be worked out overnight. Trust those whom God has placed around you during this journey and commit to traveling to the end together. As you become more vulnerable, you will get to know yourself better and you will be face-to-face with the One who knows you better than anyone else. Don't be afraid to let Him catch you as you let go of the things that have held you back in the past or the fears that crop up out of nowhere on a regular basis.

GROUP SESSION 2

Freefall
...

Welcome the group. In last week's session you learned that a freefall can be painful for several reasons. This descent requires you to face past hurts and hang-ups. It requires you to let go of all you're clinging to in order to allow God to take care of the details. It sometimes forces you to go through a painful waiting period until you find relief. But in the end, God is there to catch you if you will just trust Him. He is there to show you the life and the future He has prepared for you.

If you are willing, show your group the picture you drew in your journal of God catching you and all of your worries (p. 43). Share a little bit about the process you went through to draw and write about that.

Suggested Discussion Starters/Questions

As needed, reassure the group that as they become more vulnerable with one another, they will soon discover common ground and healing in personal weaknesses. No one should feel shame in revealing some of the ugly places that have made us stronger. And who knows … they might find they're able to laugh about their stories once they're shared!

- ☐ Have you experienced a "Camp Mom" type moment recently? What were the circumstances? (p. 32)
- ☐ How did you vent your frustrations? (p. 32)

Read Rebekah's quote on desperation at the top of page 33. Then ask a volunteer to read James 1:2-4,12.

- ☐ What struggles are you facing right now that seem overwhelming?
- ☐ Rebekah says, "God is using [our] struggles to bring about our perfection." Name one major trial you've faced and overcome. How did God help you through it? What good has come of that struggle? (p. 34)
- ☐ What things can you do to remain "steadfast under trial"? (p. 34)

Review some of the Scripture studied this week. Ask the women to get out their Bibles and read aloud the following verses as a group. Then reflect and respond to the questions that follow.

Psalm 27:13-14   Psalm 139:7-12   Isaiah 40:28-31
Psalm 37:7,34   Psalm 143:4-8   Lamentations 3:25-26
Psalm 130:5   Isaiah 30:18   Matthew 10:39

- ☐ What portion of Scripture or specific verse resonated with you during your study this week? Why?
- ☐ According to these verses, what is the benefit of waiting on and trusting in the Lord? (p. 39)
- ☐ What does waiting on the Lord look like in your current context? (p. 40)
- ☐ Which verses give you hope? (p. 40)

If they haven't already, encourage the women to write the verses that give them hope on index cards and place them somewhere they will read them often. Or take time to do this as a group activity.

Prayer & Closing

Spend some time thanking God for His sovereignty over all situations in your life and in the lives of those around you. Ask Him to speak to you as you trust Him with the outcome of whatever situation you're in. Ask Him to equip you and to teach you as you wait for him in a current situation or for one you might face in the future.

Many find comfort in isolation when difficult times arise. Often it's because you don't want to "bother" your friends with your problems or you couldn't bear for anyone to know the truth about your situation. But true community is a place where we can share our burdens without fear or shame. That kind of community takes time, so if you haven't already, make a commitment as a group that you will all take this journey together with sincerity.

GROUP SESSION 3

Naming Fears

Welcome the group. Introduce the session: Since the last group time, you have spent time naming fears, struggles, and past wounds. You faced them and brought them into the light. You learned that sometimes something has to die in order for you to live the life you were created to live. Then, you asked God to search your heart and to reveal anything that might be keeping you from having a life-giving relationship with Him.

☐ **What insights have you encountered in your study this week?**

Now lead the discussion of the Chapter 3 questions. You may draw from the following suggested questions, or if the women volunteer insights, simply guide the sharing.

Suggested Discussion Questions

☐ As a group, take some time to name some of the things we miss out on in life because of our fears, struggles, and woundings (e.g. forming new relationships, new job offers, opportunities for our spouses or children).

☐ Take a moment to review the people from Genesis and their fears and resolutions (see p. 52).

☐ Who else from Scripture can you name that overcame fears? (p. 52)

☐ What were some fears you named in your study this week (see p. 53)? What have you missed out on in life because of those fears?

☐ Pair off with someone in your group. Together, find a concordance in the back of your Bible or use an online source. Search for "fear not" and "do not be afraid" type phrases, and choose two or three verses to share with the group.

If these verses were not shared, read the following out loud: Proverbs 3:25-26; Isaiah 41:10; John 14:27; Philippians 4:6; and 1 Peter 5:7.

☐ What changes will need to take place in your life for you to believe fully the truths found in these verses? (p. 54)
☐ What other truths from Scripture and your time in study came forth this week?
☐ How are you learning to respond to God with obedience and trust?

Prayer & Closing

Spend some time reading God's Word back to Him in prayer and praise. Use the truths you have read and heard today, or speak passages that have been buried in your heart. God delights in His Word and He wants you to as well. It breathes life. It provides comfort. It gives wisdom. It is alive and active in order to guide you on your journey through life. You were never meant to walk alone. It is His very words to you.

Some of you might have shared some sensitive information today with your group. Consider this a part of the process. In order to be free, you must release something to God and possibly to others. In John 10:10, Jesus says, "I have come so that they may have life and have it in abundance" (HCSB). In order to live this abundant life, you must identify what is keeping you from living. We all have struggles, whether they were brought into the light today or kept secret in our journals. Be willing to acknowledge anything and everything to God. Be trustworthy women who hold and carry each other's burdens without finding fault or gossiping, regardless of what someone shares with the group. With true community comes brutal honesty and a commitment to confidentiality.

GROUP SESSION 4

Surrender & Rescue

...

Welcome the group. Ask what insights members have encountered in their study this week.

Take a moment to watch the video, "Being Made New," by author Rebekah Lyons, available for free at *www.lifeway.com/freefall*. Even those who have already watched the video during the session may benefit from doing so within the group.

Today, we are going to talk about what it means to surrender fully. What will it take for us to be rescued from those things that we brought to light and named. How can we live lives that reflect victory instead of defeat?

Lead the discussion of the Chapter 4 questions. You may draw from the following suggested questions, or if the women volunteer insights, simply guide the sharing.

Suggested Discussion Questions
- Talk about a time when you thought you were moving forward, only to relapse back into a previous struggle. Describe the feeling of defeat and what you did to survive (see p. 66). Ask for volunteers to also share as they feel led.

Ask a volunteer to read Psalm 139:1-6,11-12,16. On page 69, Rebekah asks, "Do you ever feel like you're just drifting through life? Do you wonder where your life is headed and what you've accomplished? Do you feel stuck on a treadmill of the mundane, working hard but not getting anywhere?"

- How do you respond to those questions?
- What keeps us from believing? What keeps us from trusting God? (p. 72)
- Why do we have trouble really believing that God will provide rest for our weary souls? That He is strong enough to lighten our loads? Explain. (p. 73)

- ☐ As a group, discuss the problems with choosing to "numb out" when we're hurting.
- ☐ What are the main reasons we would rather hide our hurts instead of share them? (p. 75)
- ☐ How can we debunk those reasons and begin the process of healing together? Be specific.
- ☐ Take time to review your life maps (see p. 77). Share some of the events and pieces of your life story that have led you to where you are and who you are today.
- ☐ As you look over your map, how have you seen God work and move in your life? (p. 78)
- ☐ At what point was He working but you couldn't see it at the time? (p. 78)
- ☐ What painful experiences turned into something beautiful? (p. 78)
- ☐ What beautiful experiences gave you the most hope and joy? (p. 78)

Prayer & Closing

Start by asking the Lord to help you as you continue to surrender to Him and to the plan He has for your life. Ask Him to reveal to you the ways He rescues you and directs you toward a more abundant life. Pray, that in the moments when you feel defeated, you set your eyes on Jesus and recognize He has beautiful experiences for your life full of hope, joy, and promise.

Remind women in the group that they each represent a unique individual who is known by God. Read Psalm 139:1-6,11-12,16 again as part of a prayer to reinforce this truth if needed. Encourage women as they dive into their study this week to remember that God wants them to live their one life well. He desires for them to fulfill the purposes of the abundant life He planned for them from the beginning (see Ps. 139:16). Challenge the women to finish the final weeks of *Freefall to Fly* with strength and perseverance by encouraging one another with texts, emails, or phone calls.

GROUP SESSION 5

One Life Well Lived
...

Welcome the group. Take a moment to watch the video, "Finding the Way," by author Rebekah Lyons, available for free at *www.lifeway.com/freefall*.

☐ What spoke to you most from the video today?

Suggested Discussion Questions
Ask a volunteer to read Matthew 25:14-30.

☐ What is the main truth you get from this passage?

☐ Describe a time when you used a gift or talent that God had given you. (p. 84)

☐ When have you "buried your treasure," or failed to use a gift or talent from God? What held you back?

☐ Rebekah asked, "Why is living in the moment so difficult?" (p. 86). Why do we sometimes live more in the past or look ahead to the future instead of focusing on the present?

☐ Name some items from your gratitude list (see p. 88). How many of these things on your list help you live more in the present?

☐ Read Matthew 6:19-21. What things did you identify to shift your focus to the satisfaction of eternal treasures instead of earthly treasures? (p. 92) How does this focus help you overcome the feeling of never having enough?

☐ Read and respond to the questions Rebekah asked at the bottom of page 95: What if my gifts are meant to illuminate my own story of struggle? What if my burden is meant to help others walk through their own difficult journeys?

☐ Rebekah wrote, "Meaning awakens when we realize our gifts. Meaning is fulfilled when our story finds purpose. Calling is where your talents and your burdens collide" (p. 97). What are your gifts? What burdens you? How do those things help you identify your purpose and calling?

☐ Describe a time you have used your burden, your passion, your heartache to help someone else. How can you do this again in the future? (p. 98)

☐ How do you see God using the talents, gifts, and burdens in the lives of others in this group? Take time to affirm one another.

Look around the room at each person present. Is someone an encourager? Is there someone who gives great advice? Is there someone who has a penchant for design? Is there someone who cooks like a world-class chef? Tell each person what you see in them and how you see God using their gifts, talents, and burdens. Sometimes we just need someone else to say out loud what we've known all along. However, God uses these affirmations as a reminder that He has something great for us and a calling that is unique.

Read Jeremiah 29:11-13.

Prayer & Closing

Ask God to guide each woman this week in the practice of being still and knowing that He is God (see Ps. 46:10) as she explores her calling. Ask Him to reveal anything that might hinder her from discovering where her gifts collide with her burdens. Praise God for what He has already done in the lives of the group members and for what He is still going to do. Ask Him to give courage to the women as they continue their journey toward a life full of meaning and complete their final week of Bible study. Remind women that God has a plan for each of them—an individual purpose and plan that no one else can fill.

You have shared many deep conversations within this group over the past few weeks. Many of you have bared your souls in a way that you've never been willing to before. As you've gotten to know yourself and those within this group on a deeper level, hopefully you also have come to know the Creator of your soul in a more deep and personal way, too.

GROUP SESSION 6

Calling & Called

...

Welcome the group. Ask what insights members have encountered in their study this week or if there is anything they would like to share from the entire study. Lead the discussion of Chapter 6 questions. You may draw from the following suggested questions, or if the women volunteer insights, simply guide the sharing.

Take a moment to watch the video, "Birthright Gifts," by author Rebekah Lyons, available for free at *www.lifeway.com/freefall.*

Suggested Discussion Questions

- ☐ After remembering portions of your past in the last six weeks through this study, what were some of your earliest hopes and dreams for your life? (p. 105)
- ☐ What were some of the major turning points? (p. 106)

Take some time to review the section "Meaning" on page 109. Review Rebekah's personal purpose statement.

- ☐ What did you create for your own purpose statement?
- ☐ How can you use that purpose to help someone else? (p. 110)

Ask a volunteer to read Ecclesiastes 3:1.

- ☐ Rebekah says, "Life exists in seasons." What season are you in? (p. 110)
- ☐ How do the purposes you are discovering mesh with the season you are experiencing?

Break into small groups. Ask each group to review the following verses and discuss the questions:

Psalm 63:1-4	**2 Corinthians 1:3-6**
Proverbs 27:17	**Ephesians 3:14-20**
Acts 1:8	**Ephesians 5:1**
Romans 12:1-5	**Philippians 2:12-16**

☐ Which verse most encourages you to live out your God-given purpose?
☐ In what ways have your life experiences prepared you to help someone else? (p. 114)
☐ In what areas do you have the most to offer in terms of Christian growth? (p. 114)
☐ Think of someone you know right now who needs to know she's not alone. Think of someone who needs an encouraging word. Choose right now to reach out to this person this week.

Prayer & Closing

Ask for specific prayer requests from the group and take
time to listen. Someone might need to share her story
right now. Pray for each spoken and unspoken request.
Ask God to give each woman a brave heart to ask for
rescue or whatever she needs at this point in life.

Today was another day of peeling back more layers of your life story. Continue to be open to what God asks you to do or say to those you come into contact with. You are His hands, feet, and voice.

Before you dismiss, make a plan to check in on each other as you wrap up this study. Although the study is over, the topics you've discussed together are open ended. Continue to find times to meet together for pure fellowship or for further Bible study. Continue to take an interest in each other's stories, and expand that to include others who need to know that their stories matter, too.

BUY THE BOOK!

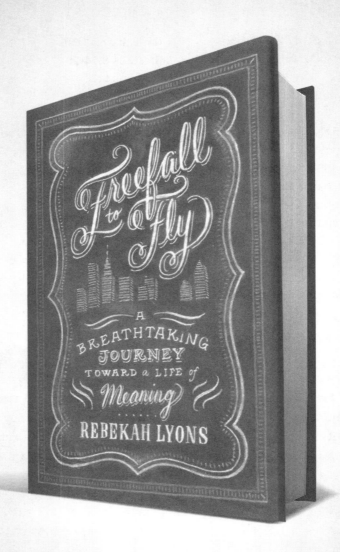

PICK UP A COPY OF THE COMPANION TRADE BOOK FOR AN IN-DEPTH PERSPECTIVE FROM REBEKAH LYONS.